May–August 2021

Day by Day
with
God

Rooting women's lives in the Bible

The Bible Reading Fellowship
15 The Chambers, Vineyard
Abingdon OX14 3FE
brf.org.uk

The Bible Reading Fellowship (BRF) is a Registered Charity (233280)

ISBN 978 1 80039 015 7
All rights reserved

Distributed in Australia by:
MediaCom Education Inc, PO Box 610, Unley, SA 5061
Tel: 1 800 811 311 | admin@mediacom.org.au

Distributed in New Zealand by:
Scripture Union Wholesale, PO Box 760, Wellington
Tel: 04 385 0421 | suwholesale@clear.net.nz

Acknowledgements
Scripture quotations marked with the following abbreviations are taken from the version shown. Where no abbreviation is given, the quotation is taken from the same version as the headline reference. NIV: The Holy Bible, New International Version (Anglicised edition) copyright © 1979, 1984, 2011 by Biblica. Used by permission of Hodder & Stoughton Publishers, a Hachette UK company. All rights reserved. 'NIV' is a registered trademark of Biblica. UK trademark number 1448790. NRSV: The New Revised Standard Version of the Bible, Anglicised edition, copyright © 1989, 1995 by the Division of Christian Education of the National Council of the Churches of Christ in the United States of America. Used by permission. All rights reserved. NLT: The Holy Bible, New Living Translation, copyright © 1996, 2004, 2007, 2013. Used by permission of Tyndale House Publishers, Inc., Carol Stream, Illinois 60188. All rights reserved. MSG: *The Message*, copyright © 1993, 1994, 1995, 1996, 2000, 2001, 2002 by Eugene H. Peterson. Used by permission of NavPress. All rights reserved. Represented by Tyndale House Publishers, Inc. TPT: The Passion Translation®. Copyright © 2017 by BroadStreet Publishing® Group, LLC. Used by permission. All rights reserved. thePassionTranslation.com. KJV: The Authorised Version of the Bible (The King James Bible), the rights in which are vested in the Crown, are reproduced by permission of the Crown's Patentee, Cambridge University Press. AMP: The Amplified® Bible (AMP), Copyright © 2015 by The Lockman Foundation. Used by permission. www.Lockman.org. ESV: The Holy Bible, English Standard Version, published by HarperCollins Publishers, © 2001 Crossway Bibles, a division of Good News Publishers. Used by permission. All rights reserved.

A catalogue record for this book is available from the British Library

Printed and bound by Gutenberg Press, Tarxien, Malta

Day by Day
with
God

Edited by **Jackie Harris**   May–August 2021

Writers in this issue

Chris Leonard lives in Surrey with her husband. They have three young grandchildren, and Chris leads creative writing workshops and holidays. She has a total of 21 books published. Find out more at **chrisleonardwriting.uk**.

Caroline Fletcher is a freelance writer. She has an MPhil in biblical studies and trained as an RE teacher. She is married to a vicar and is involved in all-age services and youth work at her church in Sheffield.

Lyndall Bywater is a freelance writer, trainer and consultant in all things prayer. She has a passion to help people get to know God better and is the author of two books for BRF: *Faith in the Making* (2018) and *Prayer in the Making* (2019).

Claire Musters is a speaker, writer and editor with a passion to see people reach their full potential in God. She has written many books, including *Taking Off the Mask* (Authentic Media, 2017). Find out more at **clairemusters.com**.

Helen Williams has worked in music, education, management consultancy and administration. She currently finds herself alongside her husband, an Anglican bishop, in some diverse contexts, while continuing to work as an accompanist.

Michele D. Morrison is a freelance writer, who loves listening for God's voice in the daily routines of life and blogging at **tearsamidthealiencorn.com** and on Facebook. She enjoys writing, playing the cello and leading Bible studies.

Amy Boucher Pye is a writer and speaker who runs the *Woman Alive* book club. She's the author of *Praying with Jesus* (CWR, 2020) and the forthcoming *7 Ways to Pray* (SPCK, 2021), among others. Find her at **amyboucherpye.com**.

Tracy Williamson lives in Kent, working with blind singer/songwriter Marilyn Baker for MBM Trust. Tracy has written several books and her latest, *A Beautiful Tapestry*, about her and Marilyn's lives and ministry, was published in November 2020 by Authentic Media.

Christine Platt has lived and ministered in the UK, Africa and Asia. She has written several Bible study booklets and devotional notes. She currently lives and worships in New Zealand and teaches English to Asian migrants.

Victoria Byrne is the seniors pastor at St Stephen's Church, Twickenham, working with older people. She is co-author of *Hope & Spice* (2018), an Indian cookbook with authentic recipes and stories of transformation from Delhi's slums, raising funds for Asha India.

Welcome

I had no idea when I sent out the commissions for this issue how the world would change dramatically in the weeks and months ahead. These notes were written during last year's lockdown at the height of the coronavirus, and many of our writers reference those events in their studies.

I had already been home-based for some weeks prior to those events, after being made redundant from my role as editor of *Woman Alive*, the magazine for today's Christian woman. As I wondered and began to pray about what next, the opportunity to become the new editor of *Day by Day with God* came as a huge blessing. And the blessings have continued.

First, it has really inspired me in my own Bible study, which I must admit had become rather hit and miss. I have been spending longer, digging deeper and rediscovering the joy of meeting God in his word.

Second, I have been able to reconnect with some of the writers I worked with previously and correspond with other regular contributors to the notes and the team at BRF. Suddenly my inbox was busy again, and everyone told me how much they enjoy writing for *Day by Day with God* and what it means to them. I'm conscious of being part of a great team.

And third, working on this issue and planning for future issues meant the lockdown days flew by, and it was wonderful to have something so positive and uplifting to focus on. These notes encouraged and challenged me as I read through them, and I am sure they will speak again as I read them with you in the days ahead.

I don't know what situations we might face this summer, but I'm praying these notes will be as much of a blessing to you as they have already been to me.

Jackie Harris, Editor

The command to be merciful

Chris Leonard writes:

When I was asked to write these notes on the command to be merciful, I said 'Yes' at once, only to realise that I'd never heard a sermon or read anything about that particular command, although it appears several times in the Bible. On the other hand, I have often read, heard, sung about and experienced God's mercy. I know, too, that God is transforming us back into his image by growing his amazing qualities within us – and they include mercy. But I found myself wondering, what does it mean for me to be merciful in the 2020s? Or, indeed, merciless?

Someone in power might exercise mercy towards a condemned criminal or enemy soldier. But that is unlikely to apply to me – or to you. A helpless maiden might cry, 'Mercy, mercy!', as the dastardly villain towers over her in some Victorian melodrama. But that's not helpful either! Modern mercy killings? Terrible, and highly controversial. Of course, there are mercy missions to disaster areas – many are God-inspired, I'm sure. But in modern, everyday English, most often the word 'mercy' appears outdated. It has top-down associations too, which is fine when applied to God, but not when it's us being merciful.

We will begin these notes by exploring what scripture means by being merciful. This is not straightforward, since at least three Hebrew and three Greek words translate as 'mercy'. The same words from the original texts translate in other scriptures as compassion, pity, love, kindness, wailing, beneficence, etc. Grace and forgiveness overlap too. Maybe grace is having what we don't deserve, while mercy means not getting what we do deserve?

It is complicated! You could see 'being merciful' as a subset of 'loving your neighbour as yourself', which is, perhaps, simpler to understand, though not to practise.

As you read the notes, it might help to ask yourself, 'What stops me from being merciful?' Things that stop me include impatience, selfishness, unwillingness to be inconvenienced and compassion fatigue. My sense of inadequacy intensifies into fear – of making things worse, or of being sucked into a huge problem and then being unable to cope. (I'll forget to take God's strength and provision into account.) I've a lot to learn – from the Bible and from our merciful God, who loves to teach and help us.

Be merciful

'[God] is kind to the ungrateful and wicked. Be merciful, just as your Father is merciful. Do not judge, and you will not be judged. Do not condemn, and you will not be condemned. Forgive, and you will be forgiven. Give, and it will be given to you.' (NIV)

We begin with the command to be merciful, given by Jesus himself to his disciples and a large crowd. It comes within a rich, challenging passage, which all boils down to a tiny word much misused in English – love. *Agape*, the Greek word here, means the selfless, giving, forgiving, compassionate, faithful, strong love at God's heart. He is 'kind' to those who don't deserve it. He is, and we are to be, 'merciful' – the word here, *oiktirmos*, means compassion. Then Jesus tells us not to judge, to forgive and to keep on giving. Mercy, like *agape* love, often requires all these active virtues of us.

I am beginning to see more clearly what the command might mean. Jesus was kind – especially to children, women and outcasts (anyone from 'unclean' pariahs to those who simply lacked status and rights within that society). Jesus had compassion on many who were blind, lame or ill, and he healed them. He had mercy on those who had done wrong and, instead of judging, forgave and motivated them to sin no more. He took compassion on hungry crowds and gave them food. He had compassion on all who were lost; he literally gave his life to bring them home to his Father again.

Any 'mercy' of mine falls way short of the mercy shown by Jesus. You too? Well, we are all 'works in progress'. I think I am less judgemental than I used to be. I rarely have problems in forgiving people, but I am aware that I don't go out of my way to be kind or even patient with certain individuals. Still, not long ago, I do remember praying hard for God's grace to be kind when I thought I wouldn't be capable of it. He answered those prayers by the bucketful and blessings abounded.

Are you, too, sensing the need to better understand and put into practice Jesus' command to be merciful? Ask for his help – and that he'll show you where, already, his grace is moulding you to be more like him.

CHRIS LEONARD

Forgive others

'Then the master called the servant in. "You wicked servant," he said, "I cancelled all that debt of yours because you begged me to. Shouldn't you have had mercy on your fellow servant just as I had on you?"' (NIV)

When the king took pity on the servant (v. 27), the word used derives from the Greek for 'bowels'. It describes the kind of compassion that churns your insides. It led here to the cancelling of all debts. That sounds like God! The word used for the 'mercy' which the servant should have shown is *eleos* (as in *Christe eleison* – 'Christ have mercy'). It means mercy, kindness, beneficence or pity. Clearly mercy, as well as love, can cover a multitude of sins!

The head of my secondary school would read this parable out loud several times a term, and I've tended to avoid it ever since. After morning assembly came 'the notices', when we'd all count how many times she would declaim, 'I will not tolerate it!' – 'it' being something like not wearing a hat on the way to school, which earnt an automatic Saturday-morning detention. 'Automatic' signified 'no appeals allowed' – hardly consistent with mercy and forgiveness!

Worse, the parable ends with the king, who represents Jesus' merciful Father, ordering that the unforgiving servant be imprisoned and tortured until he has paid his debts. Had corporal punishment not been outlawed at school, I could see our head relishing inflicting it on us. But the God I knew and loved? I struggled with that – and must admit to struggling still. Maybe Jesus was using rabbinical exaggeration to drive home the essential importance of our forgiving debts (or sins) against us. After all, what is the opposite of merciful? Ruthless? Vengeful? Almost every day we hear reports in the news of the dire consequences when individuals, gangs or nations take vengeance. Lack of mercy and forgiveness often damage many more than the perpetrator and victim, destroying swathes of God's kingdom. God will avenge wrongs – but that's his job, not ours.

'Our Father… forgive us our debts, as we also have forgiven our debtors' (Matthew 6:9, 12). Your mercy encompasses so much. Help us to receive it – and then to extend mercy, rather than bitter vengeance, to others.

CHRIS LEONARD

Give a blessing

Finally, all of you, be like-minded, be sympathetic, love one another, be compassionate and humble. Do not repay evil with evil or insult with insult. On the contrary, repay evil with blessing, because to this you were called so that you may inherit a blessing. (NIV)

Repay evil with blessing? The word is *eulogian*, meaning 'good word'. Suppose someone does or says something bad to you – call it a curse. You're merciful, replying with blessing. That's powerful to change things.

Since hearing a sermon on blessing, I am discovering the authority we're given to bless others. As God's 'royal priesthood' (1 Peter 2:9), this verse applies to each of us: 'The Lord set apart the tribe of Levi to carry the ark of the covenant of the Lord, to stand before the Lord to minister and to pronounce blessings in his name' (Deuteronomy 10:8).

Previously, if I prayed for someone's healing, rarely would much happen, but now, when God gives me compassion for someone, Christian or not, I bless them, verbally, silently or in writing, as God directs. It's been effective and well received!

The sermon came pre-Brexit, amid political tensions, distortions of truth and bitter divisions. How to pray? We were exhorted to bless leaders and influencers, that they might become what God called them to be – righteous, truthful and compassionate, working for the good of all.

Then the preacher told the story of a young man, starting his ministry in a big city in South America. As he set up sound equipment for a band, strangers approached. 'Someone wants a word with you!' They marched him to the HQ of an all-powerful drug baron, who wanted to know what he was doing. 'We'll be playing music. You're very welcome to come along.' After a surprisingly friendly chat, the evangelist asked if he might give the drug baron a blessing. Within a few weeks, the drug baron was in prison and his network permanently destroyed. Today, that evangelist leads hundreds of churches around that country. God has mercy in the ways he will have mercy!

Take up your authority in Christ today to pray blessing on someone for whom you feel compassion – or for someone who has done, or spoken, wrong.

CHRIS LEONARD

The power of grace

'You did not put oil on my head, but she has poured perfume on my feet. Therefore, I tell you, her many sins have been forgiven – as her great love has shown. But whoever has been forgiven little loves little.' (NIV)

We read a story about two debtors two days ago. Why another now, especially when the passage doesn't mention mercy? Well, as I've been saying, biblical mercy includes a whole lot more than the word in common English usage. Read through the story again, thinking about who is, and who isn't, being merciful in the wider sense. (There may be more than one person in each instance.)

Who is giving with extravagant love? Who is withholding, with contempt perhaps? Who is forgiving and who is being judgemental? Who knows they need mercy and who, being convinced that they have everything together and are in the right, feels no need of it? Who is showing compassion and who is lacking it, while sticking rigidly to the rules? Who is kind and loving and who is rejecting whom? Who is showing mercy and who is condemning whom?

Actually, I wouldn't call it mercy, because of the top-down associations. I would call it grace. God and people, rich and poor, high and lowly, old and young – all can be gracious. All of us can show grace and kindness, give, forgive – and love, of course.

Read the passage for a third time. What results from the giving and receiving of this grace, forgiveness, extravagant giving, kindness, compassion, love and mercy? We know what happened to Jesus and a little about what happened to the two debtors in his parable. But what do you think might have been the effect on the woman, who was most likely a prostitute? On Simon the Pharisee and his friends and servants who were present at the meal? On the town as rumours spread of all the outrageous behaviour (or the outrageous grace – depending on the individual's point of view)?

Are these scriptures spotlighting areas where you need to ask God for mercy, forgiveness and grace? Me too! It's a good place to start. Receive first, then give! Remember, she who is forgiven most will love most – and judge least.

CHRIS LEONARD

Widely merciful

Peter began to speak: 'I now realise how true it is that God does not show favouritism but accepts from every nation the one who fears him and does what is right.' (NIV)

If you consider that the breadth, height and depth of God extend far beyond our imagining, so does the extent of each of his qualities, like love or mercy. The early disciples had more to learn than Jesus had time to teach them on earth. Most were Jews, who had been brought up to know the God that Jesus called 'Father' as the one who had chosen their nation, ordaining special laws and customs that distinguished them from everyone else. Most hadn't understood Isaiah's prophecy about their role as a light to the nations.

Peter and Paul pioneered massive changes, having both experienced extraordinary mercy themselves. Paul, who had persecuted Christians, had his Damascus Road conversion, after which first Jesus, then courageous Ananias, showed him great mercy. Later, Paul was to write: 'Although I am less than the least of all the Lord's people, this grace was given me: to preach to the Gentiles the boundless riches of Christ' (Ephesians 3:8).

Peter had that meeting on the shore (John 21) when the resurrected Jesus mercifully reaffirmed his calling. Even then, Peter needed a vision – plus messages from Gentiles via angels – before accepting that God's mercy included Gentiles as true believers. God took all that trouble to change mindsets, so that his merciful salvation plan would be heard by the whole world!

Two things strike me. First: how fully have I received God's mercy? This mercy encompasses his forgiveness, grace, love, kindness, compassion, beneficence and faithfulness. Because, if I haven't, if I'm unsure of it, I'm not going to be equipped to extend his kind of mercy to others. It will feel too risky and I'll lack the resources. Second: what stops me from being merciful? Have I (wrongly) placed any individuals or kinds of people outside the limits of his mercy?

'There's a wideness in God's mercy like the wideness of the sea' (F.W. Faber, 1814–63). Lord, show me where I narrow your mercy, towards others or myself.

CHRIS LEONARD

Merciful boundaries

The apostles gathered round Jesus and reported to him all they had done and taught. Then, because so many people were coming and going that they did not even have a chance to eat, he said to them, 'Come with me by yourselves to a quiet place and get some rest.' (NIV)

Showing compassion to all and sundry is all very well, but sometimes we need to have mercy on ourselves – and on our families. I remember laughing at a story in an early book by Adrian Plass. The protagonist chased around helping everyone out, until his wife resorted to using a false name in a note to him. She needed his help, begging him to meet her in the local launderette (remember those?). When he turned up, eager to rescue this 'stranger', he found his wife there, struggling with piles of the family's laundry. She'd had no response in weeks of asking him to fix their broken washing machine.

While God's mercy has no limits, human strength and endurance do restrict us, even if God calls and equips us sometimes to go beyond those limits. In Mark 6 he told the weary disciples to find food in the middle of some remote desert for 5,000 hungry men, plus more women and children. But then, later in this chapter, it was he himself who blessed the small offering of food. He knew it would multiply, making plenty to satisfy and refresh them all.

If we find that we're running ourselves into the ground 'being merciful' and God is not equipping us at that level, maybe we need to ask for wisdom. It is easy to feel driven by all the need that we see, but God is not a slave-driver. He knows we won't be of much use incapacitated or dead. Moses took his wise father-in-law's advice to delegate: 'What you are doing is not good. You and these people who come to you will only wear yourselves out. The work is too heavy for you; you cannot handle it alone' (Exodus 18:17–18). Maybe God wants us to share the burden with others?

Lord, help us to come aside with you now and, within that rest and quietness, hear your wise voice showing us exactly how and where you want us to exercise mercy at this time.

CHRIS LEONARD

Merciful to whom?

'Administer true justice; show mercy and compassion to one another. Do not oppress the widow or the fatherless, the foreigner or the poor. Do not plot evil against each other.' But they… would not listen to the law or to the words that the Lord Almighty had sent. (NIV)

God cries out to his people throughout scripture: 'Be merciful to the helpless, poor and oppressed, to those who lack food, clothes or justice, to the refugee and outsider, the widow, the orphan, to those weak or sick in body, mind or spirit.' He gives promises to those who obey, such as, 'Your people will rebuild the ancient ruins and will raise up the age-old foundations; you will be called Repairer of Broken Walls, Restorer of Streets with Dwellings' (Isaiah 58:12).

Those originally sent into exile were the richer, more powerful and well-educated Jews. They had been exploiting the poor, and God was hoping the experience would cause them to repent and return to his merciful ways. Yet, after their return, most of them continued to oppress their poorer countrymen, whom the Babylonians had left behind to farm the land. The rich grabbed back the fields, charging the poor – and now landless – exorbitant taxes.

The book of Zechariah is famous for its prophecies of the rescuing Messiah's first, and second, comings, but in today's passage, Zechariah castigates the merciless returnees.

'Mercy' here is *chesed* – that 'loving-kindness' word again. It includes what I think we'd call 'social concern'. In our society the rich and powerful seem to become ever more so, while the poor, the refugees, the sick or homeless become more vulnerable and destitute. When justice goes out of the window, it's good to see individuals, churches, Christian and other organisations of goodwill, stepping up to help in different and very practical ways. One individual can't solve all humanity's problems: most can do something.

Jesus, we are now your hands and feet on this earth. Show us how and where, today, you want us to cooperate in your mercy-missions.

CHRIS LEONARD

The gift of mercy

We have different gifts, according to the grace given to each of us. If your gift is… to show mercy, do it cheerfully. (NIV)

Years ago, I ghost-wrote a book called *God's Heart for the Poor* (published by Kingsway and long out of print), about Philippa Stroud, who led a church team who helped the homeless of Bedford. This required huge sacrifices, patience, wisdom, skills and knowledge; it needed a God-given ability to love the unlovely and faith, too, that his love could save them. I became lost in admiration of what they were doing, 'But I would be useless!' I told her.

'Then your core gifting probably isn't mercy,' she replied, referring me to Romans 12. How interesting! I have prophesied but am not a prophet. I do serve, but it's not my main gifting. I teach a little, including through my writing. I give, of course. I lead writing workshops and holidays, worship services and a church home group. I show mercy in certain situations, though doubt I could do so cheerfully with the kind of people Philippa was reaching (and what desperate, homeless person wants grumpy mercy?). Maybe my core gifting is encouragement – specifically to those whose discouragement, by teachers, parents or peers, suppressed their creativity and 'voice' in expressing themselves. The point is, together we work as God's team, each with different core giftings but all supporting each other.

Those employed in the caring sector face legal, time and resource constraints. They need special gifts of mercy, together with wisdom, a phenomenal amount of energy – and our prayers. The same applies to Christian groups that are called to social concern. Treading fine lines isn't easy; it requires wise leadership. Needs can overwhelm and exhaust volunteers. Boundaries need establishing, along with support for the carers. Faith involves risk and stretches us, but it shouldn't break us or the merciful work God wants us to do.

Ask God about this quotation from Frederick Buechner in relation to yourself with regard to mercy: 'Your vocation in life is where your greatest joy meets the world's greatest need.'

CHRIS LEONARD

1 Thessalonians – holding on to faith

Caroline Fletcher writes:

Many people assume that the Bible was written a long time after the events it records and so question how much we can trust scripture. However, much of the New Testament is believed to have been composed within 40 years of Christ's death, and 1 Thessalonians was written particularly early. It is generally believed to have been written by Paul in around 50AD, less than 20 years after Jesus' crucifixion. So it offers us some fascinating insights into the world of the very first Christians.

Thessalonica was an important, populous city located in modern-day Greece. Paul visited the city with his fellow workers, Timothy and Silas, as part of his second missionary journey. You can read about their dramatic time there in Acts 17:1–15. Paul had some success in Thessalonica and several people became Christians, but it was not long before he experienced fierce opposition too. Antagonistic Jews stirred up the locals, who dragged some of Paul's new converts before the authorities and made false claims about them. Their real target was Paul, though, and he was forced to flee the city for his own safety.

Understandably, Paul was very anxious about the new believers he had been forced to abandon. They faced continuing opposition, and he was especially concerned because he had had to cut short teaching them, so he was worried their faith might not hold up in the face of persecution. However, he managed to send Timothy back to Thessalonica to find out how they were going on. 1 Thessalonians was written shortly after Timothy had returned to Paul with good news: the faith of these new believers was holding up well. However, there were some concerns. Timothy was able to report back to Paul some of the issues these believers were struggling with, much of which centred around when Jesus would return. 1 Thessalonians addresses these problems.

This letter reminds us that these first Christians did not have it easy. There is much we can learn from Paul's words to these suffering believers about remaining faithful in difficult circumstances. This letter also reminds us that this life is not all there is: one day Christ will return, and we need to be ready.

Thank God!

We always thank God for all of you, and continually mention you in our prayers. We remember before our God and Father your work produced by faith, your labour prompted by love, and your endurance inspired by hope in our Lord Jesus Christ. (NIV)

It is characteristic of most of Paul's letters to begin by giving thanks to God for those to whom he was writing. Here we see him offering up thanks for the Thessalonians' faith, hope and love, as well as their positive response to the gospel.

I'm not sure I would have started the letter this way. Being a glass-half-empty type, I have a tendency to focus on the things that need fixing. I think I would have been tempted to launch right into all the things that needed sorting out in the Thessalonian church instead of taking time to give thanks for all they were doing well. Of course, that would not have been very encouraging for them! We often underestimate what a difference praise can make to others. For example, I could not believe the change in my son when he moved from a school that focused upon what he couldn't do, to one that celebrated his achievements. The same is true for adults; taking time to recognise and appreciate what others have done well and the progress they have made can be transforming.

And by noticing and thanking God for others' achievements, we can be encouraged too. It's easy to get disheartened about the church and its failures and shortcomings. But despite its weaknesses, God is still at work among us. Progress may be slow at times, but things are still happening, and God is still changing people. By recognising how God is at work in others and giving thanks for that, our own faith can be lifted too. So, let's try following Paul's example and take time in our prayer lives to give thanks for all God has done and is doing in others.

Think of a few people you could spend time thanking God for. Try writing down a list of how God has worked through them. What about encouraging these people by mentioning some of this list to them?

CAROLINE FLETCHER

Joy in suffering

And you became imitators of us and of the Lord, for in spite of persecution you received the word with joy inspired by the Holy Spirit, so that you became an example to all the believers in Macedonia and in Achaia. (NRSV)

The Thessalonians had not had an easy time since becoming Christians. Right from the start they had faced difficulties. When Paul first brought them the gospel, some of the local Jews opposed his message and got together a mob to hunt for Paul around the city. When they couldn't find him, they dragged some of the new believers before the city authorities and made false accusations against them. These people were so full of hatred for Paul that they even pursued him to a neighbouring town.

Paul had, then, been forced to leave his new converts behind in a dangerous situation, for those who had opposed him would certainly have continued causing trouble for these new Christians in his absence. Yet despite all this suffering, Paul tells us these believers had 'received the word with joy' and were clearly still going on strongly in their faith.

I find this really challenging. It is hard to imagine being joyful in such circumstances, so how did they manage it? First, they were not surprised by suffering because they had seen what Paul himself had endured: he was their example. Christ never promised following him would be easy, but it's tempting to forget this and feel God has let us down in such times. It's important, then, to have correct expectations of the Christian life. Second, joy comes from walking closely with God. The joy the Thessalonians had was 'inspired by the Holy Spirit', not the result of their own efforts. Third, Paul had taught these new believers about all they had in Christ: God's forgiveness, his unconditional love and the Spirit's power, etc. Reflecting on these truths and thanking God for them reminds us that there is so much to be joyful about, regardless of our circumstances or how we are feeling.

Read Acts 17:1–15 for more information about what Paul and the Thessalonians had gone through. Try imagining being in their shoes, how you would have felt and how you think you would have coped.

CAROLINE FLETCHER

Courage to face our fears

Though we had already suffered and been shamefully maltreated at Philippi, as you know, we had courage in our God to declare to you the gospel of God in spite of great opposition. (NRSV)

Before Paul visited Thessalonica, his missionary journey had taken him to Philippi. There he had faced even more danger than in Thessalonica. An angry mob attacked and stripped him before beating him with rods and throwing him in prison. No wonder he talks in our passage about being treated shamefully in Philippi and needing courage to continue with his missionary journey. There are also hints in our passage that Paul's suffering was not limited to physical violence. Verse 3 suggests he had experienced false accusations against him too.

It's easy to assume Paul had the courage to keep doing God's will simply because he was a very remarkable Christian and, clearly, he was. However, Paul was not immune from anxiety. In his first letter to the Corinthians he describes being 'in fear and in much trembling (1 Corinthians 2:3) on beginning his work in that city. His courage was not man-made but flowed out of his close relationship with the Lord. Today's passage reflects this, for in it he talks of having 'courage in our God'. And Paul was not the only Christian in the Bible to be emboldened by the Lord. Remember how the disciples transformed from deserters who ran away and left Jesus at his arrest, and, in Peter's case, denied him, into leaders who preached the gospel with boldness and were prepared to suffer, face imprisonment and even die for their faith.

What do *you* need courage for? Following God will, at times, present us with challenges we fear we are not up to and we may be tempted to hold back on stepping out in faith. But be encouraged that the source of Paul's boldness was God, and the Lord can also give us the courage we need for whatever we are called to do.

What challenges do you face? Is God calling you into anything new that you are feeling anxious about? Spend time sharing with God any fears you have about these things and ask the Lord for the courage you need.

CAROLINE FLETCHER

The power of love

Just as a nursing mother cares for her children, so we cared for you. Because we loved you so much, we were delighted to share with you not only the gospel of God but our lives as well. (NIV)

I am not a great evangelist, and, like many Christians, this is something I can feel guilty about. Paul, though, was a very successful missionary responsible for spreading the gospel beyond Israel to the wider world. What can we learn from him about evangelism? Today's passage highlights a learning point that is simpler and more achievable than we might expect.

When Paul talks about his missionary work among the Thessalonians here, it is the motivation behind his evangelism that seems most important to him. It was clearly vital to Paul that he had reached out to them for good and not selfish reasons. His missionary work among them had not been done to make him feel better about himself, to impress others or to seek wealth and notoriety. What motivated Paul was the great love he had for the Thessalonians, and it is very moving to see how deeply he cared for them. Just look at the words he uses in this passage: he talks of the converts as his children whom he cared for as if he was their nursing mother and says he loved them 'so much'.

It is easy to think we will never be any good at sharing our faith because we don't have the right words to say, don't know enough about the Bible or simply aren't very confident people. Paul's example, though, encourages us that the key thing is how much we love others, for love is the most powerful form of evangelism. And this is exactly what Jesus taught when he said, 'By this everyone will know that you are my disciples, if you love one another' (John 13:35). So let's start with love, for that, more than anything else, will show people what God is like.

Spend time asking God to increase the love you have for people you know who are not yet Christians. Pray for those the Lord lays on your heart and for ways to show them God's love.

CAROLINE FLETCHER

Behaviour counts!

You are witnesses, and so is God, of how holy, righteous and blameless we were among you who believed. (NIV)

Paul may appear a touch big-headed in what he has to say in today's reading. Most of us would hesitate to declare how 'holy, righteous and blameless' our conduct has been, even if we genuinely thought that was the case! However, Paul was the subject of much criticism, and he needed to show it was groundless. He was travelling around talking about a religion most people hadn't heard of before, so people were naturally suspicious, especially as charlatans who went about from place to place teaching in order to make money out of people were commonplace at the time. It was vital, therefore, that Paul's behaviour was beyond repute, otherwise people would not believe what he had to say about the gospel, and Christianity would have fizzled out before it got going.

This is one reason why Paul worked as a tentmaker while in Thessalonica, as well as preaching. It meant he would not have to rely on others for his support and couldn't be accused of profiting financially from his preaching. He was concerned about his converts' reputations too, reminding them how he had exhorted them to 'live lives worthy of God' when among them.

Many of us will have heard people say they have been put off Christianity by the behaviour of Christians. How we conduct ourselves is important, then, for our witness. However, the reality is that none of us are perfect and we all make mistakes: lose our temper, join in some juicy gossip, say something thoughtless or unkind, etc. But even when we do fall short, we can be encouraged that if we deal with our mistakes well by owning up to them and apologising, that, too, can be a powerful witness which demonstrates God's grace at work in our lives.

Father, we are sorry when our behaviour falls short of your standards. Help us to change and become more like you, so we can be effective witnesses to those around us. Amen

CAROLINE FLETCHER

Under attack

For we wanted to come to you – certainly I, Paul, did, again and again – but Satan blocked our way. (NIV)

Today's reading is a reminder that when we seek to do the Lord's will, we may well experience opposition. First, we learn that the Thessalonian believers were being persecuted because of their newfound faith. Then, although Paul had been desperate to go and support them, he had not been able to, despite his best efforts. Paul is quite clear on the reason why, saying, 'Satan blocked our way.' He clearly believed he was in a spiritual battle that made his work for the Lord much harder. Despite being a man of God who prayed regularly and sought to do the Lord's will, his plans were frustrated.

This talk of Satan might unnerve us and make us feel fearful. However, we can learn from Paul here. He did not despair and give up on his mission because of this difficulty. Although Satan had prevented him from visiting the Thessalonians, Paul found other ways to support the church there, writing this letter and, as we shall learn later, sending his fellow-worker Timothy to see them instead. And God was at work overcoming these problems and bringing good things out of Paul's changed plans. Just think, if Paul had not experienced these difficulties, he would not have written this letter to the Thessalonians and we, as well as many generations before and after us, would have been without this powerful piece of scripture.

Paul also does not seem afraid of Satan. He talks about the opposition he was facing in a matter-of-fact way. He knew God was more powerful than the devil, for, as he would go on to write later in his letter to the Roman church, no matter what problems were thrown at him, nothing would ever be able to separate him from the love of God (Romans 8:38–39).

Paul wrote in Romans 8:28 that 'in all things God works for the good of those who love him'. Spend time reflecting on that verse and letting it speak into any difficult situations you are facing.

CAROLINE FLETCHER

Thinking of others

So when we could stand it no longer, we thought it best to be left by ourselves in Athens. We sent Timothy, who is our brother and co-worker in God's service in spreading the gospel of Christ, to strengthen and encourage you in your faith. (NIV)

At the time I write this, the coronavirus is spreading around the world, and we are seeing the best and worst in people: some offering to help their neighbours with shopping and others stripping the stores of supplies, thinking only of themselves.

The choice to consider others' needs as well as our own is a constant challenge to us all, and it was one Paul describes himself making in today's reading. After he had been forced to flee Thessalonica, he headed to Athens. He found this a particularly difficult city in which to preach. It was full of pagan worship, and many there scoffed at his teaching. In this unfamiliar and unwelcoming environment, he particularly valued the support of Timothy, a fellow worker he saw as a son.

But Paul faced a difficult choice. He really wanted to keep Timothy with him in Athens, but he was also aware that his converts in Thessalonica needed support too and he could not return to help them. So he made the tough decision to send Timothy to Thessalonica. Paul clearly struggled with this choice. The original Greek reflects his deep emotions. He did not just feel alone but also forsaken without Timothy. Paul being Paul, we can be sure he prayed over his decision, and this is the key for us too in a world of so many needs.

Being unselfish is not about simply rushing around doing everything for everyone else and becoming exhausted as a result, but involves being open to God's guidance, so we make the right choices on what to do. Paul's decision to send Timothy was clearly the right one, for he returned with good news about the Thessalonians. Similarly, God will show us, too, if we pray, how he wants each of us to consider the needs of others without becoming overwhelmed ourselves.

Dear Lord, there are so many needs around us that it can be hard to know which of them you want us to help with. Show us how to think of others without burning ourselves out.

CAROLINE FLETCHER

Praying for growth

May the Lord make your love increase and overflow for each other and for everyone else, just as ours does for you. (NIV)

When we pray for others, it can be difficult to know what to pray for, especially if we haven't been in contact with those people recently and don't know exactly what is going on in their lives. Even when I pray for people I see regularly, it's not unusual for me to feel I am just saying the same things over and over again.

Paul's prayers for the Thessalonians in today's passage give us a fascinating insight into what he prayed about, and this offers us some guidance for our own prayers. Paul's prayers were heavily focused upon the spiritual growth of the Thessalonians. First, he prayed that he might be able to visit them soon to strengthen them in their faith, as they were young converts in difficult circumstances who needed support. Then he prayed that they might grow, indeed overflow, in love for one another.

There were several Greek words Paul could have used for love, but he chose to use *agape*, a distinctively Christian word which describes an unconditional love that is given even if someone does not deserve it. This is a kind of love the Thessalonians could not simply just drum up for others; it needed to come out of their relationship with God and from his strength, especially as Paul prays they will not just have a bit of it but overflow with such love. Paul also prays that they may grow in holiness too, so they would be ready when Christ returns. Holiness involved not just being godly in their behaviour, but also having a strong relationship with the Lord.

Can we follow Paul's example and not only pray for the pressing needs of others but also for them to grow as Christians?

Try using the words of verses 12–13 in your prayers for others today, substituting in their names where appropriate.

CAROLINE FLETCHER

Unselfish sex

Each of you should learn to control your own body in a way that is holy and honourable, not in passionate lust like the pagans, who do not know God… In this matter no one should wrong or take advantage of a brother or sister. (NIV)

In today's reading Paul addresses sexual immorality amongst the Thessalonians. Sometimes the church can give the impression of being hung up on sexual sins and having little to say about wider wrongdoing such as greed, pride and selfishness. In his writings, however, Paul does not focus unduly on sexual sin alone and has a balance on this issue that today's church has sometimes lost. However, sexual immorality among his converts was a challenge Paul needed to tackle. This was because attitudes towards sex were very lax in the Greco-Roman world, and some activities that would be considered unacceptable even in our modern society were not frowned upon, including some forms of incest. In 1 Corinthians 5:1 Paul had to discipline an individual who had been sleeping with his father's wife!

It was clearly important, then, for Paul to teach his new converts that just because society accepted sexual immorality as the norm, it did not mean they should follow suit. He wanted his converts to be different. They were not to be driven by their sexual passions but should recognise that it was possible to hurt and exploit others through sex. Therefore, he warned them not to take advantage of others and wrong them in this area but to be self-controlled.

Similarly, today sex is often viewed as little more than an activity to be enjoyed, with no focus on the emotional bond it forges with another and how painful it can be if those bonds are broken. In what ways do you think sexual behaviour can be self-centred and cause hurt to others, and can sex within marriage ever be selfish and hurtful too? Can you think of examples of behaviour from other walks of life that are considered socially acceptable by many, but Christians would be wise to avoid?

Paul teaches that God takes sexual sin against others seriously. If you have ever been hurt in this way, bring your pain to God, knowing the Lord cares, brings justice and is your help.

CAROLINE FLETCHER

Serving God at work

Make it your ambition to lead a quiet life: you should mind your own business and work with your hands, just as we told you, so that your daily life may win the respect of outsiders and so that you will not be dependent on anybody. (NIV)

What do we imagine a spiritual Christian to be like? Someone who leads an extraordinary life of faith, perhaps? If that's the case, today's passage will come as a bit of a surprise. Rather than appealing to the Thessalonians to do something out of the ordinary, Paul makes a much more mundane request of them. He asks them to love each other, lead a quiet life and get on with their everyday work, so they can support themselves.

This may not seem very challenging, but there were good reasons for his instructions. It appears that some Thessalonians thought Christ would return very soon and had given up bothering to work. As a result, they were getting into financial difficulties and expecting other believers to help them out. Not only did this put a burden on their fellow Christians, but it also looked really bad to those who were not believers: they appeared lazy and irresponsible, and their behaviour must have put people off following Christ.

Sometimes we fall into the trap of thinking God only uses people who are full-time Christian workers. We also often undervalue our jobs when they are not high status or well paid. Yet Paul saw the value of working hard and carrying out our roles well, whatever they are. Greek society tended to look down on manual workers, but Paul certainly did not: he encouraged the Thessalonians to work with their hands and laboured, himself, as a tentmaker to make ends meet while in Thessalonica.

In his letter to the Colossians (3:23), Paul encourages Christian slaves to do their tasks as if they are serving God, not human masters. Similarly, whatever our roles and jobs are, if we do them well for God, then we should not underestimate what a powerful witness this can be to others.

What jobs and roles has God given you? Spend time asking God to use you in those roles and for the strength you need to do them well.

CAROLINE FLETCHER

Death is not the end

Brothers and sisters, we do not want you to be uninformed about those who sleep in death, so that you do not grieve like the rest of mankind, who have no hope. (NIV)

As I mentioned previously, I am writing this during the coronavirus pandemic. Hundreds of thousands of people all around the world have already died. Before this tragedy, I did not give much thought to death. Now it is impossible not to think about it.

In the light of this, today's reading is of huge comfort. The Thessalonians knew Jesus was to return one day and, when he did, he would take Christians to be with him in heaven. However, they had assumed this would happen in their own lifetimes. Imagine their horror when some of their number died and Jesus still had not come back. They were distraught, worried that those who had died would miss out when Jesus finally returned. The culture around them would not have calmed their nerves either, for both the Greek and Jewish faiths had little encouragement to offer about life after death, viewing it as some sort of grey, shadowy, unappealing existence, if they believed in it at all.

Paul, though, could offer the Thessalonians real hope, because Jesus had risen from the dead and so defeated death. Paul reassured them that all Christians, whether they were alive when Christ returned or not, would experience the wonders of a resurrected body and would be brought together to celebrate the return of Christ and the new life he brings.

For Paul this was not wishful thinking: life after death was something he was so sure of that belief in it gave him the strength to face dangers, imprisonments and beatings. He knew that even if his work as a missionary did lead to his death, which indeed it ultimately did, this would not be the end. And that same sure and certain hope is ours too, praise God!

Paul wrote about the last days: 'For the trumpet will sound, and the dead will be raised imperishable, and we will be changed.' (1 Corinthians 15:52, NRSV). Reflect on the wonder of those words.

CAROLINE FLETCHER

Be prepared

Now, brothers and sisters, about times and dates we do not need to write to you, for you know very well that the day of the Lord will come like a thief in the night. (NIV)

The second coming of Christ is a doctrine that has been neglected in recent years. However, it is a vitally important part of our faith. Most of us long for God to stop all the evil and injustice we see around us. When Christ returns, he will do just that, and this offers us great hope in a troubled world.

While the Thessalonians had not neglected this doctrine, some of them had become fixated on it in an unhelpful way. They were speculating about when exactly Christ would return and what this would involve. Paul believed such speculation was pointless, for no one knows these details and Christ will come back suddenly, surprising many. He said they should, instead, focus upon ensuring they were ready for Jesus' return by making sure they were walking closely with God.

And that is true for us too. Elsewhere the Bible likens Jesus' return to a bridegroom arriving for his bride. What bride on her wedding day would not make sure she was ready for the event? Imagine how a bridegroom would feel if he turned up at the church only to find his bride had forgotten the wedding was on and was running five hours late, or how he would feel if she arrived wearing some scruffy jeans and an old T-shirt because she couldn't be bothered to dress up for the special day. How would the bride feel seeing the disappointment in her loved one's eyes?

Jesus loves us like a bridegroom loves his bride, despite our many short-comings, but that does not mean we should take this for granted and be half-hearted about our faith. What do we need to do to ensure we are ready for Jesus, so when he returns, he can clearly see how much we love him?

Dear Lord, thank you that you will return and put right all the wrong we see in the world. Help me to know how I can walk more closely with you, so I'm ready when you do come back. Amen

CAROLINE FLETCHER

Different ways to love

And we urge you, brothers and sisters, warn those who are idle and disruptive, encourage the disheartened, help the weak, be patient with everyone. (NIV)

We have a cavalier King Charles spaniel called Romeo, and he could not be more different from our last cavalier, Barney. Barney was eager to please and never needed telling twice not to do something. Romeo, though, is a completely different story! No matter how often he's told not to, he keeps on trying to do the things he knows full well he shouldn't, like sneaking upstairs to chew our underwear or root through the bins. And people, too, have different temperaments, don't they? Some are extremely sensitive and can be crushed by the slightest criticism; others are completely unaffected by negative comments, even when they are more than justified.

In today's passage Paul gives the Thessalonians instructions on how to treat each other, but his words imply that different people may need to be treated in different ways. Sometimes challenging a person who is in the wrong can be more of a loving thing to do than tolerating their selfish and thoughtless conduct and attitudes. However, Paul also suggests, if someone is discouraged and struggling, then being supportive rather than pulling them up on their behaviour may be the most loving way to help them. Have a look at the advice Paul gives. Is there anyone you feel prompted to deal with differently as a result of reading Paul's words?

Paul also mentions those in leadership and talks about respecting and loving them too. It can be so easy to forget that our leaders are fallible human beings who also need support and love. We often do not know what difficult pastoral situations they are dealing with or understand all the reasons for the decisions they make, and leaders often receive more criticism than we may realise. How can you support and love your leaders?

Is there anyone you are currently struggling to deal with? Pray for God's wisdom to know how best to show love to that person and for the strength you need to do that.

CAROLINE FLETCHER

Keep coming back to God

Rejoice always, pray continually, give thanks in all circumstances; for this is God's will for you in Christ Jesus. (NIV)

We have already learned that Paul was anxious about his Thessalonian converts. They were facing opposition from those around them, so Paul gave them some instructions to help them cope in their trying circumstances.

One action he advised was to pray continually. This may seem a big ask, but what Paul was, in effect, reminding these Christians was something quite simple: to keep turning to God throughout the day, bringing their problems and concerns to him.

He was not seeking to burden them with unrealistic demands but was simply reassuring them that God's presence was with them 24/7, wherever they were and whatever they faced. He encouraged them to take advantage of this and to keep on turning to God throughout the day. Our prayers, then, don't have to be limited to the once-a-day of our quiet times. We can give over to God the things that are on our minds as we walk, as we do the housework and as issues crop up at work, etc.

Paul also advised them to give thanks in all circumstances. This, too, may seem unrealistic, but Paul knew from his own experience what a great source of strength praise was in stressful times: it was something he himself practised, for instance, when he was imprisoned. And it is so helpful because it activates our faith. Giving thanks helps us to see our situations from God's perspective rather than simply being overwhelmed by despair. The psalmists, for example, often remembered and gave thanks for all God had done for them in the past when they were in the midst of trouble, and that gave them hope and faith that God would help them in their current situations. Can you think of any times giving thanks has helped you in difficult circumstances?

Spend some time thanking God for the things he has done for you in the past and for the different ways he has answered your prayers.

CAROLINE FLETCHER

Fire and faith

Lyndall Bywater writes:

Did you ever have that irresistible urge to play with matches when you were a child? Maybe you still have it now, for that matter. Fire is a fascinating thing, and if we think that in the 21st century, with all our scientific understanding, just imagine how much more mysterious and fascinating it was to those living at the time when the scriptures were written down.

Fire must have seemed like magic. It practically springs from nowhere. It is bright, hot and unpredictable, and it can literally change the materials with which it comes into contact – or make them disappear completely. It's no wonder the ancients understood it to be a gift from the gods, and it's no wonder the people of the God of Israel believed it to be a sign of divine presence.

And fire is a helpful picture when it comes to thinking about God. It is comfort, warmth, light and safety, but it's rarely predictable and it's extremely powerful. In this modern era when we can manage so many things for ourselves, perhaps fire is the reminder we need that the God we love and serve isn't containable or programmable.

Fire appears hundreds of times throughout the Bible, and two weeks isn't long enough to do it justice, but we will delve into some of those stories to see what we might learn about God and about ourselves.

Fire often features in God's interactions with human beings, particularly when there's a calling, covenant or commitment being made. Why is that, and what does it teach us modern people who rarely get a heavenly bonfire when we respond to God's call on our lives?

Fire is also linked to punishment and judgement. What do we make of those stories where thousands die, seemingly at God's own hand?

What about suffering? That's a fire most of us have felt at some time in our lives. How do we endure the scorching of grief and pain?

And then there's that Pentecost promise that we ourselves will be baptised by fire. What does that mean, and how can we start living it out today?

As you read these stories and reflect on the truths they carry, I pray that you will know the fire of the Holy Spirit stirring in your soul, and that you will become a fire-starter for those around you.

A fiery baptism

'I baptise you with water for repentance. But after me comes one who is more powerful than I, whose sandals I am not worthy to carry. He will baptise you with the Holy Spirit and fire.' (NIV)

When I was a teenager, I bought my first 'Christian' T-shirt. It was black with rainbow writing on it, and it said: 'The next time the devil reminds you of your past, remind him of his future.' It then helpfully supplied the reference Revelation 12:10, in case you needed to check what the devil's future would be.

John did a lot of baptising. That's probably why we call him John the Baptist. But his baptism was of a particular kind. John baptised for repentance. If you went down into the desert where this eccentric prophet lived, he would ask you if you were sorry for the sins you'd committed, and then he would submerge you in the River Jordan as a sign that you were washed clean. And if you weren't sorry, there was every chance he'd preach a hard-hitting sermon that would leave you sorry!

Then, one day, Jesus arrived, and John knew a new era had been born. His job was to help people come to terms with their past. Jesus' job was to give people their future.

Today is the day we remember we've been baptised with fire. We have all made mistakes and we all need forgiveness, but we have been rescued, redeemed and set free, not just because God is endlessly merciful, but because God has a breathtakingly wonderful future for us to live. The disciples in the upper room must have had all kinds of regrets, but Pentecost was the moment when they left all that behind and set out on the astonishing adventure God had in store for them.

If you ever get a Christian T-shirt, don't get the one I got. Get one that says: 'The next time the devil reminds me of my past, I'll remind him of my future' (Matthew 3:11).

Do you ever wonder if you can be free of those old hurts and habits that make you feel dead inside? Let this truth sink in: God wants to bring you to life with the fire of his Holy Spirit.

LYNDALL BYWATER

31

A fiery reassurance

When the sun had set and darkness had fallen, a smoking brazier with a blazing torch appeared and passed between the pieces. On that day the Lord made a covenant with Abram and said, 'To your descendants I give this land.' (NIV)

> The day will come when, after harnessing space, the winds, the tides, and gravitation, we shall harness for God the energies of love. And on that day, for the second time in the history of the world, we shall have discovered fire.
>
> Pierre Teilhard de Chardin, 'The evolution of chastity',
> published in *Toward the Future*, 1936: 11

We human beings take a lot of convincing sometimes. Today's passage finds Abram in the doldrums of doubt, even though he has heard God's promise many times along his journey. In fairness to him, it has been a hard road. He has had to leave home; he's had strife in his family; he's had to fight off enemies; he's got in trouble with a Pharaoh; and now he's more perplexed than ever by a promise of descendants when he and his wife are infertile.

And it's at the end of that bad day, when the promises seem further away than ever and a life-sapping darkness has settled on Abram, that God does something remarkable. Abram has laid out pieces of a sacrifice according to an ancient covenant-making ceremony. Were this a normal ceremony, he and his partner would walk between the pieces together, as a sign of their mutual commitment to each other. But suddenly God is there, and God is 'walking' between the pieces alone. This is no 'you scratch my back and I'll scratch yours' partnership. This is the creator of all things pledging unfailing love to doubting, depressed Abram.

Why fire? Perhaps because God knew that sometimes even the most beautiful words don't break the power of darkness. When we're at our lowest, we need something warm and bright, something that lights up the darkness and banishes the cold. What we need is fire, and the truest fire is love.

Light a candle as you pray. Look at the brightness of the flame. Feel the heat which even that tiny fire creates. Then think about how much hotter, brighter and more powerful God's love must be – God's love for you.

LYNDALL BYWATER

A fiery commitment

There the angel of the Lord appeared to him in flames of fire from within a bush. Moses saw that though the bush was on fire it did not burn up. (NIV)

It is amazing what damage the two little words 'too much' can do. I have known many people who have been stifled and shut down by them: people who are exuberant in their joy and humour; people who are feisty in their quest for justice; people who are emotionally expressive in their relationships. It is heartbreaking to see their natural intensity dulled and diluted by a world which so often prefers a quiet life.

Moses could well be accused of being 'too much'. His passion for justice is explosive, whether against slave-drivers or unruly shepherds. He isn't the middle-of-the-road, safe-pair-of-hands sort of man. Read his story and you'll find an all-or-nothing man who frequently inhabits the extremes of joy and melancholy, cowardice and courage.

Yet despite his flaws, not least his spectacular lack of good judgement at times, God chooses Moses for one of the most important events in history. And the moment of choosing happens in the kind of dramatic, intense way you'd expect for a 'too much' person. There's a blazing fire on a hilltop in the desert, a ritual removing of shoes and then a blazing argument.

God made Moses. God knows exactly what kind of encounter Moses needs to have if he is to trust and follow God. Though Moses has to learn wisdom and moderation along the way, God never asks him to damp down his intensity or shut down his passion. In fact, God appears to Moses in blazing fire and searing heat, matching his intensity and mirroring his passion.

If anyone has ever implied that you're 'too much', just remember Moses and his encounter with the one who appears as fire, whose passion for justice is a white-hot blaze and whose intense, steadfast love burns brighter than the sun.

God, you love us intensely and completely. Forgive us when we tone ourselves down to fit in, or when we make others tone themselves down to keep the peace. Help us be fully the people you made us to be.

LYNDALL BYWATER

A fiery approval

The angel of God said to him, 'Place the meat and the unleavened bread on this rock, and pour the broth over it'… Then the angel of the Lord touched the meat and bread with the staff in his hand, and fire flamed up from the rock and consumed all he had brought. (NLT)

My first guide dog was a golden retriever/Labrador with an opportunistic streak, especially where food was concerned. She'd use all her cunning and agility to steal whatever she could, then consume it completely, so she could try to persuade you it had never existed in the first place. One day, my family left her at home alone with a freshly baked lemon meringue pie (albeit pushed to the back of the kitchen worktop). When they returned, she greeted them with the tin foil case in her mouth, a wagging tail and a broad Labrador grin on her face. It was her seal of approval.

Gideon is having the strangest of days. He is so frightened of the occupying power that he's threshing wheat in a winepress (a sort of big box), and suddenly he's being told he's going to lead a liberation army. In his awe and utter discombobulation, he makes a loaf of bread out of an ephah of flour – that's about 36 pounds or 16 kilograms! When he brings his huge loaf, his meat and his gravy to God as an offering, God's response is to consume the whole lot with a burst of warm, bright fire.

I suppose Gideon could have been offended, seeing as he'd worked so hard – and probably used up all the family's flour supply – but he wasn't. Perhaps that's because he knew the story of Abram and the story of Moses. He knew that when God shows up in fire, it's a sign of love and a seal of approval.

God's words to Gideon were about heroism and warfare, but God's sign to Gideon was love. Whatever you're called to, whatever brave things you know God is asking you to do, never forget that the first and most important thing you are is loved.

Do you ever feel like God is your boss? Do you ever find yourself measuring your value by your successes or your achievements? God welcomes your offerings of service and obedience, but he burns with love for you.

LYNDALL BYWATER

A fiery vote of confidence

Then Manoah took a young goat, together with the grain offering, and sacrificed it on a rock to the Lord. And the Lord did an amazing thing while Manoah and his wife watched: as the flame blazed up from the altar towards heaven, the angel of the Lord ascended in the flame. (NIV)

The day before we opened our first prayer community premises in Canterbury, we went to the building to make final preparations for the move, only to find that someone had tied red balloons to almost every lamp post in the street. There was no sign of a party anywhere, and no indication of why the balloons were there. We thought nothing more of it until the next morning when we returned to find all the balloons had gone except the one on the lamp post right outside our door. Humanly speaking, it was just a coincidence, but to us it felt like more than that. It felt like God's blessing on our new venture, and our logo has been a red balloon ever since.

Manoah and his wife have been given quite a task. They are to go from being infertile to raising a son who will become a Nazirite prophet of God. It's no wonder Manoah feels the need for a crash course from the angel. And when he does get the instructions, the job probably seems even more daunting than before. Who are they to do this important thing for God?

It's then that God does something beautiful with fire again. It's not quite the same as with Moses or Gideon. This time it's Manoah who starts the fire, but it's the angel of the Lord, that precious manifestation of God's presence in our human world, who accepts those flames as his transport to the skies. That's quite some vote of confidence! It's no wonder the couple end up face-down in wonder.

God has every confidence in you. The angel of the Lord may not appear in the flames of your barbecue anytime soon, but no matter how inadequate you may feel, know that God believes in you.

How might it change your feelings and your attitudes if you were certain God had confidence in you? Have you ever experienced something which felt like God giving you a vote of confidence?

LYNDALL BYWATER

A fiery presence

By day the Lord went ahead of them in a pillar of cloud to guide them on their way and by night in a pillar of fire to give them light… Neither the pillar of cloud by day nor the pillar of fire by night left its place in front of the people. (NIV)

My spiritual growing up was something of a rollercoaster experience, not because anything truly dreadful happened, but because my moments of encounter with God were rare but extremely powerful. Much of the time I was serving faithfully with little sense of connection, but several times a year I'd end up at a summer camp or a big event, and suddenly the near-ness and love of God would overwhelm me. That experience would carry me for a few weeks, until I slid back down to 'normal'.

The pillar of fire is a sea-change for the Israelites. They know the stories of Moses and Abraham. They know that when God wants to show up in love and power, there's likely to be fire involved, but it's always been moment-ary – a one-off experience to be wondered at, pondered on and consigned to memory. Imagine their amazement then when the cloudy, fiery pillar turns up and doesn't disappear… for 40 years! God isn't just going to pop in and check on them a few times a year at the big festivals; God is on the journey with them.

Yet they grumble, complain, rebel and get frightened. They talk of having been led out into the desert to die. Surely these aren't the secure, confident attitudes of people who know they're in the company of the divine. The truth is that we humans have a tendency to live as though God isn't with us.

How often do you find yourself giving way to fear, wallowing in loneli-ness or feeling you've been abandoned? We may not get a fiery pillar to look at, but the presence of God with us is fact – every moment of every hour of every day. The challenge for us is to remember it and live like it's true.

Lord, I'd love a pillar of fire, so bright and obvious wherever I go. Yet you are with me, around me and within me, more real than the air I breathe. Help me to tune my awareness to your presence.

LYNDALL BYWATER

A fiery faithfulness

'Command the Israelites to bring you clear oil of pressed olives for the light so that the lamps may be kept burning… Aaron and his sons are to keep the lamps burning before the Lord from evening till morning. This is to be a lasting ordinance among the Israelites for the generations to come.' (NIV)

I have an entire cupboard full of candles I haven't got around to burning. I love candles and I receive lots, but I am hopeless at remembering to get them out and light them. Most of the time they sit dormant and cold in the cupboard, then a few times a year I make a concerted effort and have a big 'burn-out'. Come to think of it, it's rather similar to my spiritual life.

The God of fire instructs the Israelites to keep a lamp burning every night. While the pillar of fire burns outside, the menorah will burn inside, and the work of keeping it burning is theirs, not God's. The people will supply the oil and the priests will keep the wicks alight. Compared to the vast column of fire at the head of the camp, it's a tiny lampstand, but it's an important part of their relationship with God, which is why it's given as 'a lasting ordinance… for the generations to come'.

We love the idea of being 'on fire' for God, but it's easy to assume that's God's job – to set us ablaze for an exciting faith journey. While it's true that God gives us the oil of his Spirit, it's entirely up to us whether that oil is ever ignited in us or whether, like my many candles, it languishes in a dusty cupboard.

What does ignition look like? Paul suggests it's something to do with using our gifts. 'Fan into flame the gift of God, which is in you through the laying on of my hands' (2 Timothy 1:6). We so often wait for the fire before we use our gifts, but what if it's using our gifts that ignites the fire in us?

If you're feeling flat and flameless today, why not do something you know you're good at? Each time you choose to be the person God made you to be, you put a spark to the Holy Spirit oil within you.

LYNDALL BYWATER

A fiery terror

Mount Sinai was covered with smoke, because the Lord descended on it in fire. The smoke billowed up from it like smoke from a furnace, and the whole mountain trembled violently. (NIV)

In the Australian summer of 2019–20, a land area of over 46 million acres was burnt by bush fires. Almost 10,000 buildings were destroyed, and a number of people lost their lives. Fire can be deadly.

Over the past week, we've read stories of God appearing in fire, bringing comfort, reassurance, affirmation, hope and love, but we'd be missing something if we didn't spend some time looking at those stories about God being the fire that threatens to consume and destroy.

I confess I find passages like today's challenging to read and even more challenging to understand. God seems angry. That warm, loving presence seems to have turned dark somehow. Yet perhaps that's just my automatic assumption. We humans are hardwired to fear anger, maybe because it so often comes laced with barbs of unkindness – even hatred. We rarely manage to be angry without being unloving, and so we fear anger when we encounter it in others.

God certainly sounds angry here, but what might the Israelites hear if they can listen beyond their fear? Might they hear the voice of one who is aggrieved at the state of a broken world and who must express that grievance, but who doesn't want them to get hurt in the process? Might they hear a warning to stand back and let the divine furnace roar because sometimes it must?

I sometimes wonder if I'd feel safer with a God who doesn't get angry. I don't believe God's wrath manifests in bush fires, but I do believe it's real and I find it scary. But then I reflect on the many things in this world that are wrong, unjust, even evil, and I have to conclude that anger is a necessary energy. I need to be free to get angry, and so does God.

Is there an injustice which makes you angry? Has it ever occurred to you that God might burn with anger about it too? As you pray, speak your feelings and then ask the Holy Spirit to tell you God's heart.

LYNDALL BYWATER

A fiery disaster

Aaron grabbed the censer, as directed by Moses, and ran into the midst of the congregation. The plague had already begun. He put burning incense into the censer and atoned for the people. He stood there between the living and the dead and stopped the plague. (MSG)

This is the story of a disaster. I've heard plenty of theological acrobatics to explain why the deaths of many thousands of people was somehow God's will, but it's never sat well with me. This was a dark day when rebellion, plague, earthquake and fire killed far too many innocent people.

'He is the Rock, his works are perfect, and all his ways are just. A faithful God who does no wrong, upright and just is he' (Deuteronomy 32:4, NIV).

The word 'just' means 'fair'. God is absolute fairness. It is not possible to be fairer or more just than God. So, if you read today's story and think it all seems rather unfair, there's every chance God agrees. If you read today's story and wonder how God could be rageful enough to send an earthquake to swallow up entire families (including children) and a fire to consume 250 people, even though they'd chosen to step away from the rebels they'd been associating with, then you're on to something. It may help to know that, for those who recorded these stories, there was no other explanation for disaster than God being angry. If the crops failed, God was angry; if a baby died, God was angry; if a nation conquered another nation in war, God was angry with the losers and on the side of the winners. Put like that, it sounds crazy, doesn't it? Yet that kind of thinking still rears its head from time to time, even in our day.

There are three lots of fire in this story: fire carried by the rebels, fire that destroyed the 250 erstwhile associates and fire in Aaron's hand that stopped the plague. In all that chaos, perhaps it was just that final little fire that held the merciful presence of God.

Lord, in a world beset by disasters, both natural and man-made, I thank you today for the fire of your mercy. In Jesus, you stood between the living and the dead, turning the tide of disaster; turning despair to hope.

LYNDALL BYWATER

A fiery refining

He'll be like white-hot fire from the smelter's furnace. He'll be like the strongest lye soap at the laundry. He'll take his place as a refiner of silver, as a cleanser of dirty clothes. (MSG)

The year 2020 will long be remembered as the year we encountered Covid-19, a virus which locked us down, changed our ways of doing things and stole far too many lives. It will be many years before we truly understand the impact this pandemic has had on our world. Yet it has also been a refining. For a time, all sorts of air-polluting activities had to stop – things like air travel and car travel – and we had to change the way we gathered and interacted with each other, forcing us to think about what really matters.

God isn't a vengeful tyrant who spews out fire in a fit of rage, but this Malachi prophecy warns us that a day will come when wickedness will be exposed and brought down. God may not be a petulant despot, but neither is God a disinterested bystander. When evil, selfishness and injustice scorch our lives with their fire, God is there, present with us in the flames, using the heat of suffering to release some new goodness into the world. God will act, and fairness and justice will have their day.

Burning stubble in a controlled way leaves the soil more fertile. Refining precious metals leaves them purer. Applying heat can help to clean and restore things. Are you feeling the heat of suffering just now? Are you struggling to understand how God could have allowed what you're living through, or whether it might be God's will for you? Love never wishes ill on another, but love can't always stop the harm others choose to do us, or the many bad things that happen in a fallen, broken world. Yet love will never leave you. Love will rise over you like a sun, hotter than any furnace of suffering, bringing healing, restoration and hope.

Is there a work of refining going on in you? Are you having to make difficult choices or let go of precious things? How might you cooperate today with the refining work which love is doing in your life?

LYNDALL BYWATER

A fiery tempering

Then King Nebuchadnezzar leaped to his feet in amazement and asked his advisors, 'Weren't there three men that we tied up and threw into the fire?… Look! I see four men walking around in the fire, unbound and unharmed, and the fourth looks like a son of the gods.' (NIV)

If you want to make metal more resilient, there are two things you need to do. First you harden it by heating it to a very high temperature and cool it quickly by dipping it in cold liquid. That makes it hard, but it also makes it brittle, meaning it cracks or shatters easily, so you then need to temper it. Tempering is a similar but slower, more controlled process of heating and cooling which leaves the metal tough but slightly softer, so it can stand greater pressures without breaking.

On the day Nebuchadnezzar throws Shadrach, Meshach and Abednego into a super-heated furnace, they're already pretty hardened. Having served in the Babylonian court for a long time, they know the shifting moods of its power-crazed kings and they know how far they'll go before refusing to toe the line. Their willingness to die in the furnace shows the hardness of unyielding faithfulness to God.

But perhaps the furnace proved to be a place of tempering. They go into that fiery hellhole not expecting to be rescued. They go in because they believe it's the right thing to do. But while they're in there, they meet with the living God. It's the angel of the Lord again, the presence of God in human form. Some might even call him Jesus. And those who have walked with Jesus in the fieriest of hellholes are not just brave and hard; they're also enduring and resilient.

The furnace of suffering can harden us. It can leave us brave but brittle, easily cracked by pain or shattered by disappointment. But it can also temper us if we meet Jesus in it, leaving us softer and more resilient, confident in the knowledge that we can always trust him to walk with us through even the worst experiences.

Have you been through suffering which has hardened you and made you brittle? Are you aware that the experience has left you fearful or fragile? Talk to Jesus about it, asking him to bring comfort and peace as you remember.

LYNDALL BYWATER

A fiery proving

The quality of materials used by anyone building on this foundation will soon be made apparent, whether it has been built with gold, silver, and costly stones, or wood, hay, and straw… because it will be revealed by blazing fire! And the fire will test and prove the workmanship of each builder. (TPT)

When I was young, a kind man bought me a cuddly tiger cub. I was sad because I'd left my favourite cuddly toy at home, and he bought me the tiger because he knew it would cheer me up. Tigger remained a firm favourite for the rest of my childhood. That little incident happened almost 40 years ago, and I've never forgotten it.

Whether it's the good we do, or the good others do for us, good will always last. Peter talks about the fire of suffering proving that our faith is made of solid stuff. If you've ever been through times of real doubt or heartache and yet you're still walking with Jesus, you'll know exactly what he means. Your faith may not be as simple and shiny as it was when you were younger, but it's somehow more real and more precious than ever.

Paul talks about how the good we do for others lasts. Like the precious metals in his list in 1 Corinthians 3, the good things we do are precious, and no amount of suffering or judgement will ever be able to destroy them. If we spend our energy on things that have no eternal value – things like popularity contests and pointless debates – we'll have little to show for it in the end, but one act of pure kindness can stay in a person's heart for a lifetime.

The trouble is, you only prove how solid and lasting something is by going through the fire of trials. It's the difficult times that show you how precious and strong your faith really is, and it's the difficult times – like when you've left your favourite cuddly toy at home – that give other people the chance to do good, kind things for you which you remember for ever.

Have you done something which you know has blessed someone deeply? Is there a facet of your relationship with God which has become more real because of a difficult experience you've been through?

LYNDALL BYWATER

A fiery troublemaker

The tongue also is a fire, a world of evil among the parts of the body. It corrupts the whole body, sets the whole course of one's life on fire, and is itself set on fire by hell. (NIV)

'Sticks and stones may break my bones, but words can never hurt me.' That's how the rhyme goes, at least, and it's no wonder it's a children's rhyme, because I don't know an adult in the world who would agree with the sentiment.

In the course of these studies we've thought a lot about fires which involve the presence of God, fires which come as a result of our broken world and fires which test our faith, but we must also give thought to the destructive fires which we ourselves can start.

Yesterday we reflected on the idea that good things always last, but sadly that's not to say that bad things never do. If you've ever had something truly hurtful said to you, you'll know how difficult it is to get it out of your mind. It can undermine you for years, popping up just when you thought you'd forgotten it and destroying your confidence all over again. Perhaps that's why James has such dark things to say about the tongue. With just a few words, we human beings can spark fires that burn for decades.

The trouble is, words seem so transient. Surely, if we do say something hurtful, we can just undo it later by saying something nice? It's interesting that James is so appalled by the idea of the same tongue speaking bad and good words. Perhaps it's because he knows that words aren't transient. They come out of the beliefs we have and the attitudes we hold. If our hearts are critical and negative, so will our words be. If our hearts are generous and loving, so will our words be.

Fortunately, it's entirely possible to start good fires with our words too – fires of courage, self-confidence, hope, joy and love in those around us.

Lord, I offer you my tongue today. As I speak with people, show me any negativity in me which might cause me to speak an unhelpful word. Help me to choose words which start the right kind of fires.

LYNDALL BYWATER

A fiery baptism

Suddenly a sound like the blowing of a violent wind came from heaven and filled the whole house where they were sitting. They saw what seemed to be tongues of fire that separated and came to rest on each of them. (NIV)

There's a story from the tradition of the Desert Mothers and Fathers which has always caught at my heart. Abba Lot goes to Abba Joseph to ask what more he can do for God, beyond his duties of fasting, prayer, study and repentance. Abba Joseph reaches his hands skyward, spreads his fingers like ten lamps and says, 'If you will, you can become all fire.'

On this final day of our exploration of fire in the Bible, we come full circle to Pentecost again. The fact that the disciples were touched by tongues of fire isn't just a nice, comforting image. It's the warning and the invitation to us to become all fire.

The trouble is, we hear those words and immediately think we should be performing miracles every day, changing the world before breakfast or undergoing some major personality transplant. But what have we learnt over these past two weeks?

We've learnt that fire is God's language for steadfast, unconditional love, so we can blaze up straight away by loving well. We've learnt that God adds fire to the things we offer – our gifts, our talents, even our quirky baking experiments – so we can start doing the things we're good at and trust God to ignite them. We've learnt that God refines and strengthens us when we go through the fire of suffering, so we can trust the process even when it hurts. We've learnt that we can start fires with the words we use, so we can look for opportunities to ignite hope.

I certainly wouldn't rule out the miracles, by the way. Life with God is an adventure, and being 'all fire' may just surprise you from time to time, but there are plenty of ways to embrace the fiery life, even before the signs and wonders begin.

Lord, I so often let my Christian life become cold and dry. I settle for ticking boxes instead of soaking in the flammable oil of your Holy Spirit. Help me trim my wick so I'm ready to blaze for you.

LYNDALL BYWATER

Ordinary imagery, extraordinary God

Claire Musters writes:

Throughout the Bible, God used the most ordinary people and their every-day tools and gifts to do extraordinary exploits for him (such as David with his sling and stone). Jesus also used ordinary, everyday items to perform his miracles (think of how he turned water into wine and used mud from the ground to heal a blind man).

I would like to encourage you to start looking out for the holy within the ordinary. The Bible has many examples of that too – for instance, in Exodus 3:1–3 we read that Moses met with God… through a burning bush. But that bush was just a normal bush, one Moses would have passed by over and over again. It was simply transformed when God's presence came on it (as we can be too).

We are going to concentrate on the images used to describe God and what they teach us about him – and us. We can learn a lot about God's character from unpacking scriptural descriptions, such as a potter, a mother hen or a rock. We can also understand more about our relationship with him, for example, where Zephaniah describes God singing over his people.

Jesus often used ordinary imagery to describe himself so that his listeners could connect with and understand what he was saying to them. For example, when he called the first disciples, who were fishermen, he told them to leave their nets as he would make them 'fishers of men'. Through everyday language, he expressed precisely what they would spend their lives doing through evangelism, discipleship and, ultimately, martyrdom. He also used very visual language, which helps us to grasp complex subjects (such as him being the vine and his Father the gardener).

God's love, delight and care for us are shown through scripture in many everyday ways: when Elijah was exhausted and fearful after the showdown with King Ahaz and the prophets of Baal, God used ravens to bring him food. And then he came to him – not with a fanfare, but in the silence (1 Kings 19:11–13). May we, too, find time to come before God in silence, with open hearts to hear from him. I pray that these notes may help you to think about, and connect with, God in new ways.

The master potter

Yet you, Lord, are our Father. We are the clay, you are the potter; we are all the work of your hand. (NIV)

The book of Isaiah is a message of judgement for both Israel and Judah, the two kingdoms which formed the nation of Israel. They had been unfaithful to God and the prophet Isaiah received visions that showed both judgement and salvation.

The chapter we are focusing on describes how fearsome God's presence can be – 'You came down, and the mountains trembled before you' (v. 3) – and yet Isaiah recognised that this awesome God still cares for us (vv. 4–5). He pleaded with God not to remain angry with his people, who continued to sin, but also included this highly evocative picture of God being the potter and his people the clay.

Interestingly, this comes straight after his acknowledgement that God is our Father. Don't most parents, out of love, try to mould and shape their children so that they grow up to be responsible adults? This imagery speaks to me of God being fully in control and us being moulded by his hands – even when we are being disobedient. And yet it also reveals the depths of his love: think how messy the process of being at a potter's wheel is – God is happy to get his hands dirty in order to make us more like his Son.

Isaiah's prophecy reveals that God is both fearfully awesome, controlling all of destiny, *and* kind. Just as a potter works hard to create an item of beauty, God is at work in our lives, moulding and shaping us each day. Clay can crack easily, and yet a master craftsman works patiently and methodically until the finished article is revealed.

Thank God for continuing to take the time to mould you, even when the process has been painful. Ask him to make you aware of his potter's hands in your life today.

CLAIRE MUSTERS

A God who weaves

My frame was not hidden from you when I was made in the secret place, when I was woven together in the depths of the earth. (NIV)

As we will see with today and tomorrow's reflections, God is sometimes described using imagery traditionally associated with women. I find this hugely uplifting, as it reminds me that I, too, as a woman, am made in the image of God.

I love Psalm 139. It is one of the passages I come back to time and time again, particularly when I'm doubting my identity. The knowledge that God knew me before I was born, knows all the days I will spend on earth but, more than that, actually weaved my body together is so incredible, but also comforting.

The verse often cited is, 'You created my inmost being; you knit me together in my mother's womb' (v. 13). In other versions, the word knit is replaced with 'wove', and, indeed, the original word used means 'to weave together'. This is reflective of the way women in biblical times used a loom to clothe their family.

In her book *Image of the Invisible* (BRF, 2019), Amy Scott Robinson paints a beautiful and vivid picture of what that would have been like. A typical home would have been very modest, but somewhere there would have been a home-made loom. Throughout her day, the woman of the household would pause from the sweeping, cooking, cleaning and washing she was doing to send the loom's shuttle back and forth. A garment would grow over hours, days – until she was ready to start a new one.

This was an everyday part of life; something the rest of the household barely noticed. And yet it took skill and planning, as the weaver decided on the pattern and length of the item. In the same way, God works away in the secret place, weaving together new life in an expectant mother's womb. How mind-blowing.

Lord, I thank you that you place such attention to the details that are unique to each of us; your love and care is incredible. Amen

CLAIRE MUSTERS

Like a mother bird

He will cover you with his feathers, and under his wings you will find refuge. (NIV)

There are many instances of God being described as a bird, with us finding protection and comfort from hiding under his wings. The psalmists use this imagery when they are facing battles, when their enemies are closing in and they feel the need to cry out to God to hide and protect them.

This idea of God covering us with his wings is, again, quite a feminine image, which Jesus himself acknowledges in Matthew 23:37: 'Jerusalem, Jerusalem... how often I have longed to gather your children together, as a hen gathers her chicks under her wings, and you were not willing.' This verse expresses the deep desire he has to look after us. But how often do we pull away, as my teenager does when I try to embrace her? We might feel we are too independent to need that kind of care, as she does, or we might long to stay hidden under God's wings.

Deuteronomy 32:10–11 continues the metaphor, but also reveals that God will nudge us forward when it is time for us to take flight, 'like an eagle that stirs up its nest and hovers over its young'. That 'stirring' often involves making the eaglet uncomfortable, by bringing food less often and removing the lining material from the nest. All this disruption makes the young desperate and pushes it to try out its wings – and then, it discovers that it can fly. Sometimes the way God works in our lives can seem bewildering, as he encourages us to stretch the wings of our faith. However, as verse 11 goes on to show, God doesn't just leave us to fall. Like the parent eagle, God remains with us (even if we aren't aware of him) and when we need him to, he will catch us.

Thank you, Lord, that you know better than I know myself when it is time to flex my faith muscles afresh. Help me to trust that you will not leave me to fall – but will help me to fly. Amen

CLAIRE MUSTERS

Singing over us

He will take great delight in you; in his love he will no longer rebuke you, but will rejoice over you with singing. (NIV)

The context of this verse is within a prophecy, similar to the one that Isaiah shared, but this time Zephaniah is speaking to Judah (about 40 to 60 years after Isaiah). The people were still rebelling, still worshipping foreign gods. But, yet again, after a horrific description of judgement, we see the hope of restoration bursting forth. And it is at this point that we hear that God takes delight in his people and, rather than rebuking, loves to sing over them.

Singing is such a wonderful, stress-relieving pastime. There is a lot of singing in our household: my husband used to be a record producer, so music has always surrounded us, and I head up our worship team at church. Both our children are musical too, and so, although they are a lot more private now they are pre-teen and teen, can be heard singing around the house. I love it when my daughter joins in with worship practices and sings alongside me in church services. I also find that it's when I'm singing in the shower that inspiration for writing or speaking comes, too.

Singing is something I hold very dear. And so, to know that God sings too is both wonderful – and ordinary. It is something we can all do and glean pleasure from whenever we want to. But how awesome to know that God likes to sing too – and that singing over us is something that gives him pleasure.

I like to imagine him drawing close to me and singing love songs that reach down into my heart, giving me a sense of acceptance and affirmation. Rather than the love songs so many (talented) songwriters produce each week, how wonderful to imagine God partaking in songwriting that is about us personally.

Take some time today to simply stop and visualise God singing songs of love over you. You might want to ask him to share with you the words that he is singing.

CLAIRE MUSTERS

God our rock

The Lord is my rock, my fortress and my deliverer; my God is my rock, in whom I take refuge. (NIV)

God is described as our rock in various places in the Bible, most often in the psalms. There are verses that declare he is our rock, a firm place for us to put our feet.

I love Psalm 18:33 – 'He makes my feet like the feet of a deer; he causes me to stand on the heights' – as it reminds me of my son. When we visit my dad, he loves the chance to go down to the beach and clamber on the big rocks. While I can find them slippery, he darts about just like I imagine a deer would, totally confident that he will remain sure-footed. This is what God does for us when we place our trust in him. When we build our lives on him, we can be assured that he will be a trustworthy foundation. As Jesus explains in the parable of the wise and foolish builders (Matthew 7:24–27), hearing from God and obeying his direction for our lives is like building on a foundation of rock, rather than sand.

Other writers in the New Testament reveal that Jesus is the rock. In 1 Peter 2 we are told he is the living cornerstone (on which those of us who believe are being built), and in 1 Corinthians 10:4 Paul tells us that Jesus is the rock that Moses struck with his staff in Exodus 17:5–6, providing much-needed nourishment to the Israelites in the desert.

Interestingly, some of the imagery in the psalms refers to the rock as a military metaphor. For example, in Psalm 144 when God is called 'my Rock', David goes on to say that he 'trains my hands for war'. The metaphor of God as rock shows his strength, but also how he provides strength for us too.

God, I thank you that I can build my life upon you, knowing that you are my rock. You provide a sure footing for me, as well as strength and power for the day ahead. Amen

CLAIRE MUSTERS

Jesus the Nazarene

**'Nazareth! Can anything good come from there?' Nathanael asked.
(NIV)**

As we turn now to the New Testament, let's remind ourselves of how lowly a background Jesus had. Not only was he born in a stable, but he also grew up the son of a carpenter in the town of Nazareth. As we see in today's passages, Nazareth was looked down upon by the Jews. It was a small town, but it housed the Roman garrison in charge of the area around Galilee. Perhaps because of this outside influence, Nazareth was viewed as having a somewhat independent spirit and a reputation for poor morals and religion. It was into this lowly town that God's Son was placed. However unlikely, this ordinary, looked-down-upon town housed an extraordinary man.

The passage in Matthew indicates that this fulfilled what had been foretold by the prophets, which speaks to me of God's heart for using the unexpected and unlikely. The heart of Jesus revealed a willingness not only to lay aside his privileged, divine position to come to earth as a human, but also to be located in a place that he knew would cause people not to believe who he was. Indeed, later on he again experienced scorn from his hometown, as they wouldn't accept the miracles he was doing. Jesus explained: 'A prophet is not without honour except in his own town and in his own home' (Matthew 13:57).

When I read about Jesus' ordinary, humble beginnings, I am filled with hope. When I feel weak, when I feel looked past and so feel useless, I remember that he also chose me. I may well not be as strong and influential as others, but we read in 1 Corinthians 1:27: 'God chose the weak things of the world to shame the strong.'

Lord, thank you for your willingness to be made so lowly. Whenever I compare myself to others and feel I fall short, or feel overlooked, help me to remember I have been chosen by you. Amen

CLAIRE MUSTERS

The vine and gardener

'I am the vine; you are the branches. If you remain in me and I in you, you will bear much fruit; apart from me you can do nothing.' (NIV)

This passage has been one of my favourites since childhood. I love the rich, clear imagery of Jesus being the true vine and us being the branches. As those of you who are gardeners will know (and please excuse the rough-and-ready description – I am not a gardener!), plants need pruning in order to produce flowers or fruit in the next season.

Vines being grown outdoors in the UK are mainly pruned in early winter, but the training and pinching of new shoots, and the thinning out of fruits, happens in spring and summer. The main pruning can look quite vicious – such as cutting main stems right back to simply leave two strong buds.

Knowing God is the gardener means we can trust his hand even when it feels like our lives are being heavily pruned. I know this from experience. There was a time when my life fell apart around me, and everything was taken away before being built back up. (This was due to my own sin, so God was shielding me from the bad fruit that would have been produced. I explore this in *Taking Off the Mask*, published by Authentic.)

There was another, more recent, time in which I was continuing to do what I thought was much good ministry. But God had been asking me to slow down and I hadn't been listening. When we are doing things out of our own strength, the fruit is not as good as it could be. He forced me to stop through (fairly minor) ill health, until I allowed him to direct what needed pruning and what should be allowed to flourish.

Take some time to sit before God, imagining your own branch within the vine. Are there parts of it that have got tangled, or have begun to wither rather than produce fruit? Yield yourself to the gardener afresh today.

CLAIRE MUSTERS

The bread of life

'I am the bread of life. Whoever comes to me will never go hungry.'
(NIV)

A great crowd of people had gathered to hear from Jesus because they had seen him perform miracles. And yet most were without food. Jesus knew what he was going to do and the lesson that he could teach out of the resulting miracle. When asked what provisions there were, Jesus was shown a young boy's ordinary lunch of bread and fishes. He used such meagre, ordinary means to feed the whole of the crowd (cited as being 5,000 men, but as this did not include women and children there may have been thousands more).

The next day, the crowd followed Jesus to the other side of the lake. Having fulfilled a physical need, he now had the opportunity to open up the conversation to the spiritual. The crowd brought up the miracle of God feeding the Israelites manna from heaven (see Exodus 16), but Jesus then said something remarkable: 'I am the bread of life.' His listeners would have been familiar with the way God fed the Israelites: it was miraculous, but they had to rely on fresh manna for each day, as any leftovers went bad overnight. It was a step of faith, but also a matter of life or death out in the desert.

Bread is an everyday, staple food that we use to stave off hunger pangs. Jesus related himself to this ordinary product but transformed it into the extraordinary: if we accept the bread that God offers to us (Jesus), we will never go hungry again. By using the image of bread, Jesus was also referencing his sacrifice: bread is broken in some way, usually sliced, in order to be consumed. This is reminiscent of the way his body was broken for us on the cross.

Next time you eat some bread, reflect on the fact that Jesus described himself as the bread of life. Thank him for his daily sustenance and take time to symbolically accept it (you might like to take Communion).

CLAIRE MUSTERS

The good shepherd and gate for the sheep

'I am the gate; whoever enters through me will be saved... I am the good shepherd. The good shepherd lays down his life for the sheep.' (NIV)

Jesus was speaking directly to the Pharisees (teachers of the Jewish law), who were often among the crowds that gathered around him and were aghast at his teaching because they felt he was being blasphemous.

Jesus told them that he is the gate, the right way into the sheepfold. Shepherds often gathered their sheep into folds at night-time to protect them from wild animals, thieves and the weather. These folds were often simply caves or open areas that had been cordoned off using walls of stones and branches, etc. Jesus was explaining that, unlike false teachers, he is the way to know God – the way into God's sheepfold. Not only that, but he is also the good shepherd who, like shepherds did with their sheep, would put himself in danger to keep his sheep safe.

This metaphor was powerful because people would not only have understood the work of a shepherd, but also would have made the link between what Jesus was saying and Old Testament prophecies. For example, in Ezekiel 34:15–16 God called himself the shepherd – 'I myself will tend my sheep and make them lie down' – and in verse 23 we see a prophecy regarding the Messiah: 'I will place over them one shepherd.' This angered some of Jesus' listeners, but, today, we can take great comfort from the level of care Jesus describes.

Jesus also told the parable of the lost sheep (see Matthew 18:12–14; Luke 15:3–7), which reflects what God says in Ezekiel: 'I will search for the lost and bring back the strays. I will bind up the injured and strengthen the weak' (v. 16). These promises were not just for his followers then – he is still our good shepherd today.

Jesus, I thank you that not only are you the way to eternal life, but you also tenderly care for our needs once we are part of your flock. Amen

CLAIRE MUSTERS

The Lamb of God

'Look, the Lamb of God, who takes away the sin of the world!' (NIV)

John the Baptist had been chosen by God to prepare the way for Jesus and, when he spotted Jesus coming towards him, he declared that Jesus was the Lamb of God. This metaphor of an ordinary, everyday creature was loaded with meaning, and those with spiritual ears to hear would have begun to make the connection.

In the Old Testament we see the Israelites were taught to sacrifice a perfect lamb twice a day to atone for their sins (see Exodus 29:38–42). When Abraham was asked to sacrifice Isaac, we read that God provided a ram to be sacrificed in his place (see Genesis 22), which was a foretaste of what Jesus would do for us all (prophesied also in Isaiah 53:7). The act of the very first Passover (see Exodus 12) and all subsequent sacrifices fore-shadowed his once-for-all blood sacrifice, and Jesus is referred to as the Passover lamb in 1 Corinthians 5:7.

Having been crucified and then raised from the dead, Jesus is now seated in the heavenly places. An incredible picture of him as the worthy Lamb of God was given to another John when he was exiled on the island of Patmos: 'Then I saw a Lamb, looking as if it had been slain, standing at the centre of the throne, encircled by the four living creatures and the elders. The Lamb had seven horns and seven eyes, which are the seven spirits of God sent out into all the earth' (Revelation 5:6). Jesus is no longer the meek, silent lamb who allowed himself to be killed by human hands; he is the only one worthy to take the scroll – and the only one worthy of our worship today!

Lord, I marvel that John saw you as the Lamb – with both humility and majesty. I thank you for your willingness to be sacrificed on my behalf. Help me to live with these images in mind today. Amen

CLAIRE MUSTERS

Water of life

'Whoever drinks the water I give them will never thirst. Indeed, the water I give them will become in them a spring of water welling up to eternal life.' (NIV)

As we saw with the very vivid metaphor of Jesus providing more long-lasting sustenance than the bread used in the miracle of feeding the 5,000, this passage echoes a similar sentiment. However, this time Jesus used something even more necessary for sustaining human life: water.

While we can go for a prolonged period without food (scientists have no definitive length but say around three weeks), we can only survive a matter of a few days without water. This is because it is so fundamental to our beings – we are around 60% water, after all. We also excrete water throughout the day through sweat and urination, and so need to replenish our levels.

The woman at the well was there because of necessity. She had chosen a time of day when most would be hiding from the heat – perhaps because she was shunned by society and so didn't have much choice. She needed the water. But, having given her some dignity by speaking to her directly (which men didn't normally do with women, and certainly not a Jew with a Samaritan), Jesus revealed that he could offer water that would never run dry.

In other places in the Bible, God is referred to as the fountain of life (Psalm 36:9) and the spring of living water (Jeremiah 17:13). Incredibly, this metaphor was revealing Jesus as the Messiah. The woman misunderstood his message to begin with, thinking she wouldn't have to draw from the well each day, but by the end of the passage Jesus spells it out more clearly for her (see v. 26).

I wonder whether we view spending time with Jesus as vital as drinking water. And I wonder how often we intentionally draw on the well of living water he has placed inside of us.

Next time you reach for a glass of water, pause and think about the living water that Jesus has given you. Drink deeply physically but also spiritually, thanking him for his refreshment.

CLAIRE MUSTERS

Jesus the servant

Jesus knew that the Father had put all things under his power, and that he had come from God and was returning to God; so he got up from the meal, took off his outer clothing, and wrapped a towel round his waist. (NIV)

Jesus and his disciples had entered Jerusalem for the Passover festival. The timing was significant. Jesus knew his time to be sacrificed was near, and so he took the opportunity to love and teach his disciples something fundamental. Having shared the last supper together, and already knowing that Judas would betray him, Jesus did something extraordinary – because it was so lowly and ordinary.

Jesus positioned himself as a servant and washed his disciples' feet. In biblical times, there would have been a servant positioned at the ready when guests arrived at someone's house. Wearing sandals while walking along dusty roads, which would also have been full of animal excrement, it was a necessity for people to have their feet washed when entering a house. What a horrible job for the servant!

By washing his disciples' feet, Jesus was aligning himself with a lowly position. It is worth mentioning here that when Jesus described himself as a shepherd, that, too, was an incredibly lowly job. Jesus had to explain to his disciples more than once that his is an upside-down kingdom: 'Whoever wants to become great among you must be your servant, and whoever wants to be first must be your slave – just as the Son of Man did not come to be served, but to serve, and to give his life as a ransom for many' (Matthew 20:26–28).

Imagine what it must have been like for Jesus to kneel in front of Judas, and to tenderly take his feet, washing the dirt away. And try to comprehend how that must have made Judas feel too. Now put yourself in front of Jesus. Will you allow him to wash your feet or (like Peter) is your first response indignation (see v. 8)?

Lord, help me to accept your offer to wash me clean each day. And help me to have the same servant-hearted attitude towards others. Amen

CLAIRE MUSTERS

Our bridegroom

'How can the guests of the bridegroom mourn while he is with them?' (NIV)

In the Old Testament, God had already referred to himself as a bridegroom – describing the joy that he would have in his people (Isaiah 62:3–5). The prophet Isaiah had spoken of God's judgement, but also his salvation, and there are many Messianic references within his book. So it follows that Jesus would also refer to himself as the bridegroom. The above quotation is taken from the verses in Matthew. John's followers had gone to Jesus and asked why his disciples were not following the customary rules for fasting. Jesus indicated that, while he was with them, it was time for them to feast.

This image of Jesus being our bridegroom continues right through to the end of the Bible. In Revelation 19:7–9 we see that the world's history is wrapped up with the wedding of the bride of Christ (the church) to the Lamb – another reminder that we can only enjoy this incredibly intimate relationship because of his sacrifice.

Revelation 19:7 talks of the bride having 'made herself ready'. A wedding only happens because both parties have chosen to make that commitment. God has shown his incredible love towards us throughout history (and the overarching story of the Bible). As we await Jesus' return, when he will come back for his bride, are we making ourselves ready?

Paul, writing to the church in Corinth, spoke about his desire to be able to present them as pure to Jesus: 'I am jealous for you with a godly jealousy. I promised you to one husband, to Christ, so that I might present you as a pure virgin to him' (2 Corinthians 11:2). Do we have that same desire for ourselves and those around us? What are you doing to ensure that you are ready for Jesus and remaining holy for him?

Lord, the image of you as the church's bridegroom teaches me of your tender and unwavering love and commitment to me. Help me to stand strong against other desires that seek to turn me away from you. Amen

CLAIRE MUSTERS

The head of a body

Now you are the body of Christ, and each one of you is a part of it. (NIV)

Yesterday we looked at our close relationship to Jesus, as the church is his bride. Today's metaphor takes our role even further. Colossians 1 indicates that Jesus is the head of the body, but that body is each one of us! The passage in 1 Corinthians says, 'Just as a body, though one, has many parts, but all its many parts form one body, so it is with Christ. For we were all baptised by one Spirit so as to form one body' (vv. 12–13). Those who belong to Jesus are part of his body here on earth, and have a vital role to play – isn't that incredible?

As this text indicates, none of us has any right to look down on another because they are different to us – each part of the body is vital, and that is how Jesus views us. This is a call to unity, but also to action. Jesus is the head of the body, which means he directs and guides (as a brain does within a human body), but as the hands, feet, arms, legs, stomach, toes, etc., we need to actually move in order for his will to be done here on earth.

As we come to the end of our look at the ordinary imagery used to describe our extraordinary God, it is also extraordinary that he should choose to use you and me to outwork his purposes. And what a great rebuttal for the negative thoughts that can sometimes enter our minds, telling us we are not as useful as others around us! Remind yourself today that 'God has placed the parts in the body, every one of them, just as he wanted them to be' (v. 18).

Lord, I thank you that you chose me to be a part of your body, and that you created me exactly as I am. Help me to celebrate that, and play my part just as you want me to. Amen

CLAIRE MUSTERS

Lydia: a woman of valour

Helen Williams writes:

I see a lot of purple in my life – I am married to a Church of England bishop who has shirts, cassocks and suitcases in various shades of purple! A woman who knew all about the colour purple is the woman we meet in Acts 16, 'a dealer in purple cloth', known as Lydia. Luke writes only seven sentences about her, but his words provide more personal detail than we have about any of the other characters he introduces us to in his book. In preparing these notes, I have read imaginative novels and informed but speculative commentaries about her. The truth is that we know very little, but what we do know, and can sensibly surmise, is both fascinating and challenging for us as 21st-century women.

We meet Lydia around AD52 in the Roman colony of Philippi in the north-east of Greece. Philippi, named after Alexander the Great's father, was famous not only for its goldmines, but also as the site of the battle where Julius Caesar's murderers were killed in 42BC. 'We'll along ourselves, and meet them at Philippi,' says Cassius grimly to Brutus in Shakespeare's play, as they prepare to face Mark Antony and Octavian for their final show-down. Philippi was also a cannily strategic place to live as a trader, as it was on the Via Egnatia, the ancient trade route linking Europe and Asia.

This was not Lydia's home, though. Home for her was Thyatira, across the Aegean Sea, in what is now Turkey. Thyatira was a multicultural city renowned for its huge proliferation of creative guilds and particularly for its cloth-dyeing industry. It is probable that Lydia (possibly a widow) moved from here to Philippi to extend the family business out into Europe. Whatever her role, she was clearly a successful, independent and wealthy woman, working in a luxury, high-end market.

How and why the Holy Spirit got her into position in Philippi, leading her to the place of prayer down by the River Gangites on that particular sabbath morning for an encounter with the living God, is the subject of our week's reflections. The way he barred doors and opened others to Paul on his second missionary journey, to ensure he was at the same place at the same moment, is quite remarkable! I've loved delving into the background of this story, and I hope you do too.

Guide me, O thou great redeemer

Paul and his companions travelled throughout the region of Phrygia and Galatia, having been kept by the Holy Spirit from preaching the word in the province of Asia… They tried to enter Bithynia, but the Spirit of Jesus would not allow them to. (NIV)

One afternoon recently I set off on my usual local walk, turning left out of the drive, but something stopped me in my tracks, so I set off in the opposite direction – not a sensible idea, as it was nearly dusk and the walk this way would entail walking along a lane with rush-hour cars and limited visibility. Within ten minutes, though, a person loomed out of the twilight, walking towards me. It was someone I knew, and she was in some distress. She would never have wanted to bother me, and she told me she'd never walked that way before! I joined her and we talked and prayed through some of the things troubling her.

On a rather different scale, how God arranged things so that Paul would be in the right place at the right time to meet Lydia is brilliant! Setting out from Antioch, Paul and Silas had travelled to Derbe and Lystra, picking up Timothy on the way. Bizarrely, the Holy Spirit then prevented them from preaching in Asia. We can imagine Paul's frustration, as he is forced to abandon his grand plan and turn off to Phrygia and Galatia. Then it happened again: reaching the border of Mysia, they tried to enter Bithynia and God said, 'No', so they ended up in Troas.

When the call came, it was clear and unequivocal because it was in a dream – the plea of a 'man of Macedonia'. Doors had banged shut, but now it was time for the Holy Spirit to open the right door. The following morning the missionaries must have discussed the dream (the word 'conclude' (verse 10) is *symbibazo* in Greek, a collaborative verb meaning to 'bring together'). How they must have chuckled when they realised that the harbour at Troas faced west towards Macedonia!

You know when you have a brilliant idea, but God has other plans in mind? Four principles guide us here: use your common sense; watch where God opens and closes doors; ask for revelation and consult Christian friends.

HELEN WILLIAMS

Pay attention

We sat down and began to speak to the women who had gathered there. One of those listening was a woman from the city of Thyatira named Lydia, a dealer in purple cloth. She was a worshipper of God. The Lord opened her heart to respond to Paul's message. (NIV)

It was Paul's custom to seek out the synagogue whenever he arrived in a new city. It seems that there weren't the requisite ten Jewish men in Philippi to form a synagogue, and so Paul and his team are directed outside the city walls and down to the River Gangites, where a group is meeting to pray. The Greek word Luke uses here means 'prayer house'. Jews of the Diaspora would often build these in riverside locations, convenient for baptisms and ritual washing. This sabbath morning the group seems to comprise of women, and Luke homes in on an Asian woman (which is ironic, given that Paul was prevented from preaching in Asia!) who is glued to Paul's words and hungry for his message.

To Lydia's credit, it is impressive that as a wealthy businesswoman, head of household and away from home, she still determines to keep the sabbath and pray. We assume that she had embraced the Jewish faith back home in Thyatira (where there was a thriving Jewish community) and become a proselyte, though she was probably not of Jewish descent. She clearly integrated prayer into her life, though, and Luke notes she is a 'worshipper of God'.

As far as she understood, Lydia loved and served God, but as she listened, 'the Lord opened her heart'. It is a wonderful moment when her faith moves from her head to her heart! Chrysostom, an early Church Father, said of this encounter: 'To open is the part of God and to pay attention that of the woman.' Paul's way of sharing the gospel was perfect for this intelligent woman whose life was devoted to beautiful things. He simply and quietly 'sat down' and told her about the Beautiful One. It was quite different from the God-encounters others in Philippi were to have.

Why not ask God to open your heart today? It is easy for faith to get stuck in our head and not impact our very being. I love the words of the poet Mary Oliver: 'Pay attention. Be astonished. Tell about it.'

HELEN WILLIAMS

Holy encounters

Immediately he and all his household were baptised. The jailer brought them into his house and set a meal before them; he was filled with joy because he had come to believe in God – he and his whole household. (NIV)

And so, a wealthy businesswoman from Asia becomes the first person on the continent of Europe to meet Jesus Christ and give her life to him. Paul had been called to Philippi by a Macedonian man, but the Holy Spirit leads him first to a woman, a woman who will play a significant part in planting the first Christian church in Europe.

Before looking at Lydia in more depth, I invite you to step back for a moment and look at the full description of Paul's visit to Philippi. The context for Lydia's story is so exciting. Luke, our narrator, by the way, seems to be a genuine eyewitness at this point. In verses 10–39, he uses the pronoun 'we'. His return to 'they' in verse 40 suggests he may have stayed on in Philippi when the others left, probably helping the church to get established.

After Lydia, it is a demon-possessed, Greek slave girl who has a transformative encounter with the living God. Though we clearly see Jesus' resurrection power at work here, this represents economic disaster for her exploiters. Paul and Silas are duly arrested, but God does something miraculous, even through the incarceration, turning a potential suicide into another powerful encounter with himself. This time, it is a Roman jailer, probably a retired army veteran who is overwhelmed by meeting a greater king than Caesar.

You may well know that every morning the head of a Jewish household would thank God that he was not a Gentile, a woman or a slave. How thrilling that the first European converts are a woman, a slave and a Gentile! We could hardly imagine a more disparate group, each of whom meets Jesus in a way perfectly fitting for them, and it's with these three that the European church is founded.

'There is neither Jew, nor Gentile, neither slave nor free, nor is there male and female, for you are all one in Christ Jesus' (Galatians 3:28). Jesus spoke so compellingly about unity. Let's pray for Christian unity in all our diversity.
HELEN WILLIAMS

The colour purple

Here's the reward I have for every conqueror… You'll rule the nations, your Shepherd-King rule as firm as an iron staff, their resistance fragile as clay pots. This was the gift my Father gave me; I pass it along to you – and with it, the Morning Star! (MSG)

Tyrian purple garments, textiles and soft furnishings were the preserve of the wealthy elite in Lydia's day. The dye was highly prized because its colour didn't fade but actually became brighter with exposure to sunlight. No wonder it was so pricey, though: to make it, it literally thousands of marine snails (murex) had to be harvested and boiled in giant lead vats for several days. The smell, not surprisingly, was terrible! Even 12,000 snails would only yield 1.4 g of pure dye! Very few could afford this luxury. The togas of senior Roman magistrates might be edged with this purple, but it was only a triumphant general who could wear a full purple robe.

Lydia's hometown of Thyatira was renowned for the production of this dye and other dyes too. Inscriptions have been found in the city referring to the guild of dyers. In fact, Thyatira, it seems, had more guilds than any other Roman city in Asia. There were woolworkers, linen workers, makers of outer garments, leather workers, tanners, potters, bakers and bronze-smiths. Lydia grew up in this highly creative setting and clearly developed a gift for producing and marketing her beautiful luxury fabrics.

It's fascinating then that, when the Holy Spirit addresses the church in Thyatira through John in Revelation 2 (somewhere between 17 and 43 years later), he uses expressions like 'feet of furnace-fired bronze', 'firm as an iron staff' and 'fragile as clay pots'. He is speaking to the hearts of crafts-people through their own medium. While he praises the love, faith, service and persistence of the Christian community, there is a serious warning about being misled and diverted from the truth. Most importantly though, Jesus offers himself to them in the beautiful metaphor of the Morning Star (compare 22:16) – the source of light, clarity and truth.

I'm reminded of the old Salvation Army hymn: 'Let the beauty of Jesus be seen in me, all his wonderful passion and purity. O, thou Spirit divine, all my nature refine, till the beauty of Jesus be seen in me.'

HELEN WILLIAMS

A different way to live

Meditating on things true, noble, reputable, authentic, compelling, gracious – the best, not the worst; the beautiful, not the ugly; things to praise, not things to curse. Put into practice what you learned… and God, who makes everything work together, will work you into his most excellent harmonies. (MSG)

It seems that Lydia was not only aesthetically aware and a product of the artisan city she came from, but she must also have been a feisty business-woman. Talking to the theologian, Paul Thaxter, about Lydia recently (while in Uganda), he pointed out to me that she 'offered an alternative model to the Empire of slavery', running her family business capably and ultimately bringing her whole household with her on her journey of faith. We assume this means children as well as male and female slaves (the Greek word for 'household' strongly suggests it) and that they all 'bene-fited from [Lydia's] gospel, enterprise and initiative'. This stands in stark contrast to the position of the poor slave girl, who was probably 'trafficked, exploited and treated as property' in an 'economic system based on abuse which seemed to benefit only men'. Go, Lydia!

'The Lydian Woman' (perhaps only a trade name alluding to her origins in Lydia and not her real name) was clearly known and respected around Philippi, owning a large enough villa to invite Paul and his team to stay (with no deference to a man, which is why we assume she was a widow). Indeed, we read in verse 40 that the Christian community met in her house. She was no doubt one of the 'holy people' to whom Paul wrote his letter not long after this. Philippians 4:3 makes special mention of the women, and, as we read Paul's letters, we realise that Philippi was alone among the young churches in its generous giving. I love to think that as Lydia had received Jesus, she in turn modelled the gift of generosity to this young community, putting into practice what she had learned of grace and watch-ing God work her 'into his most excellent harmonies'!

Some of us are businesswomen; some are not. God's call to each of us is to be what he has made us to be. 'Whatever you do, work at it with all your heart, as working for the Lord' (Colossians 3:23, NIV).

HELEN WILLIAMS

Come and stay!

Love each other as if your life depended on it. Love makes up for practically anything. Be quick to give a meal to the hungry, a bed to the homeless – cheerfully. Be generous with the different things God gave you. (MSG)

Today is St Lydia's day in the Russian Orthodox Church, which holds her in high regard as 'equal to the apostles'. Lydia must have played a significant part in leading the new church in Philippi after Paul's departure. She is certainly one of the feistiest people we read of, challenging Paul and winning (Acts 16:15). After her heart is opened to Jesus, she persuades her household to join her in following him and they are baptised together in the river. Her next priority is to invite Paul, Silas, Timothy and Luke to stay at her home, and she won't take 'No' for an answer. 'If you consider me a believer in the Lord,' she pleads, 'come and stay at my house' (Acts 16:15, NIV). How fearless she must have been in business!

We see this same courage later in the chapter, as Paul and Silas are released from prison and make straight for her house. She seems unafraid to be associated with the Christian cause or troubled by any potential scandal. Hosting meetings where a new Jewish Messiah, and not an emperor or pagan Roman god, was worshipped could have ruined both her reputation and her business.

Hospitality throughout Acts seems to play a vital part in the spread of the gospel. If you have time, do look at these examples: Simon the Tanner (9:43); Peter (10:23); Cornelius (10:48); Mary (12:12); the jailer (16:34); Jason (17:5–7); Aquila and Priscilla (18:2–3, 26); Titius Justus (18:7); Philip (21:8); Mnason (21:16) and Publius (28:7). 'Be generous with the different things God gave you,' says Peter. Hospitality doesn't have to be lavish but, in these times, when opening our homes to each other is less and less common, it can take courage to offer something welcoming but simple. I'm sure Lydia has something to teach us about this.

Ask God if there's any way you might use your home or resources to help someone this week. See if God puts someone on your heart – it may end up being something as simple as asking them for coffee.

HELEN WILLIAMS

A woman of valour

She is clothed in fine linen and purple... She makes linen garments and sells them, and supplies the merchants with sashes. She is clothed with strength and dignity; she can laugh at the days to come. She speaks with wisdom, and faithful instruction is on her tongue. (NIV)

We cannot leave our encounter with Lydia without considering her Old Testament prototype: the woman described in this 22-line poem (an acrostic in which every line begins with a different letter of the Hebrew alphabet). I wonder if you, like me though, come to this passage with slightly gritted teeth. We have often felt like it was a task list for The Perfect Woman. Irritatingly, Lydia seems to fit the model well. She is a successful trader; an efficient manager of her household; I am sure she wore the purple cloth she sold; and we know her to be someone who feared the Lord.

The thing about this poem, though, is that it was written for men to sing in praise of women (v. 31), rather than to make them feel inadequate. I think the writer's mother wanted him to notice the multitasking women so often do, the glory there is in the everyday. It works on another level too, as a celebration of wisdom, almost saying, 'This is what wisdom in action looks like.'

It is interesting to note too that the phrase 'noble character' seems to miss the point of the Hebrew word, which has much more to do with valour or strength. This changes things. Wherever you find yourself today – rich or poor; single or married; in work or out; at home or away; whoever you are, whatever you do, be a woman of valour.

Lydia was a pretty extraordinary woman – ahead of her time, independent, feisty and successful, but, far more importantly, she was diligent in worship; open to God; willing to change and expand her horizons; and, having met her Lord Jesus, someone who then went on to share her faith publicly and privately, opening her home to host and grow the first Christian church in Europe.

Lord, you know my circumstances today. In them I want to be a woman of valour. May I be 'clothed with strength and dignity', laughing 'at the days to come', speaking 'with wisdom' and with 'faithful instruction' on my tongue.

HELEN WILLIAMS

Caring for God's creation

Michele D. Morrison writes:

Greta Thunberg, the Swedish teenager whose impassioned appeals for action to slow climate change inspired a global movement, said: 'Adults keep saying, we owe it to the young people to give them hope. But I don't want your hope… I want you to panic.'

And many people are panicking. In a 2017 report, the American Psychological Association described the impacts of climate change on mental health as 'eco-anxiety', defining that as 'a chronic fear of environmental doom'. Eco-anxiety does not anticipate redemption, but destruction.

I am writing these notes while self-isolating. The Covid-19 pandemic drove a tsunami of panic-buying, leaving shelves as bare as a field after locusts have swarmed. Panic-buying is a symptom of deep fear and a sense of helplessness. It reveals a selfish urge to ensure I and my loved ones survive.

The staggering speed at which the virus swept the world illustrates our global interconnectedness. We need to work together to halt environmental degradation and reverse its effects. How interesting that as people self-isolate, air quality improves and wild animals flourish. Was there ever a clearer or more indisputable illustration of the effect of human behaviour on the environment?

Do not be afraid, God says. Panic, an extreme form of fear, freezes us. Hope, however, hope resting in God, is a confident expectation that God is good, faithful and in control. In Jesus, he has already redeemed creation. Believing that truth is the antidote to despair and also the call to actively partner with God to bring about change.

God doesn't want his creation spoiled. He wants us to be his hands and feet, working with him to husband the world effectively, compassionately and lovingly. I hope that as we walk through these next two weeks together, we will refresh our vision of God's intention that humanity is responsible for working with him to care for the earth. May that renewed vision inspire creative thinking and determination as we lead and join with others to remediate pollution and enable restoration of the natural environment.

'The Lord reigns, let the earth be glad; let the distant shores rejoice' (Psalm 97:1, NIV).

By his grace

The earth is the Lord's, and everything in it, the world, and all who live in it; for he founded it on the seas and established it on the waters. (NIV)

This is a psalm of ascent, probably sung by David and the Israelites as they carried the ark of the covenant up the hill to the place where it would reside, where Solomon would build the temple. It is a song that celebrates God's ownership of the earth, which he established on the waters. Waters are not stable. They are subject to tides and currents; they are tossed by winds and earth tremors. Why would God establish his earth on the seas? Perhaps this small detail reminds us that although we are made to live in harmony with creation, we are to respect and care for the earth without revering it. Historically, many civilisations have deified creation, and today there are those who worship the created rather than the creator.

Jesus told a story of a wise man who chose to build his house on rock, rather than on shifting sands. As stewards of creation, we are to be diligent with its care, but the only sure foundation for our lives and our faith is the rock of ages, Jesus Christ, who guides our stewardship.

Lest we become overwhelmed by the problems facing us as we seek to remediate the destruction we have wreaked on the environment, let's pause to reflect on our own limitations and throw ourselves on the unlimited grace of God. As we trust in him, his grace and mercy refresh and renew us. Our prayers for help, and our recognition that without him we can do nothing, are key to creation care.

The Lord our God is mighty to save – not just people, but the planet, too. The earth is the Lord's and he has a plan for it. We need not panic.

Oh Lord God, help me not to lose heart as I see the vast destruction of habitats and resources. Help me to throw myself into obeying you, trusting in your power and wisdom to turn things around.

MICHELE D. MORRISON

In the beginning

In the beginning was the Word, and the Word was with God, and the Word was God. He was with God in the beginning. Through him all things were made; without him nothing was made that has been made. (NIV)

My husband Don is an artist. I have often watched him regard something with careful concentration and then proceed to recreate it, getting the proportions right, the angles right, the colours right. One holiday, our rental apartment was owned by a potter, who offered the use of clay and kiln to those who wanted to try their hand at pottery. Don worked in the art room for hours, creating a fanciful cottage complete with crooked nose and friendly smile. When I wipe the window ledge on which it rests, I take care not to bump or drop it, as it reminds me of that fun day in France, with the man I love. I want to preserve it.

John tells us here that Jesus, the Word, is the creator God. Everything was made through him. Nothing has its source in anything other than God. In Genesis we read that day by day, at creation, God regarded what he had made and concluded that it was good.

Anyone who has stood on tiptoe at the edge of the Grand Canyon, snorkelled above the Great Barrier Reef or watched a vivid sunset or a bright rainbow cannot but conclude that this earth is stunning. Look at the long-necked giraffes and the perky meerkats and see God's smile. Watch elephants show each other affection; see the devotion in your dog's eyes as she looks at you, and you feel the love the creator has for his creation.

When I look at the natural world, my heart joins with all creation to sing a praise to the God who created it, the God whom I adore. And the last thing I want to do is spoil his handiwork.

Father, Son and Holy Spirit: the beauty of the Trinity relationship is clearly seen in the beauty of the creation. Thank you, Lord, for your outstanding, awesome gift of the world, and the privilege we have of stewarding it.

MICHELE D. MORRISON

Window on the almighty

For since the creation of the world God's invisible qualities – his eternal power and divine nature – have been clearly seen, being understood from what has been made. (NIV)

It has been said that science and faith are incompatible. In recent years, however, as cutting-edge research has revealed the incredibly precise tuning of our planet to allow life to exist at all, a growing number of scientists have found God in their discoveries.

Dr Allan Sandage was a 20th-century American astronomer whose observations of distant stars showed how fast the universe is expanding and how old it is (13 billion years or so). He credited science as being the driving force behind his midlife conversion to belief in God as the creator. 'If there is no God,' he said, 'nothing makes sense.'

God reveals himself in his creation, both to those of unscientific mind who simply appreciate its vastness, its precision, its beauty and detail; and to those who can answer questions of how, what and when but have to shrug or turn to God to answer the question of why.

'What may be known about God is plain… because God has made it plain' (v. 19). If we see the loving face and personality of God when we look at creation, how terrible is it if we willingly mar his face by exploitation and reckless neglect? Christians stroll through God's world with him as a companion. How can we, then, of all people, brazenly spoil his creation?

Some of our actions stem from ignorance. Until recently, perhaps, we didn't think about the way our throwaway lifestyle generates mountains of waste, often shipped to emerging economies which may have no choice but to accept our garbage. Thoughtlessness – using a car when we could walk or cycle, wrapping something in single-use plastic when we could store it in a reusable container – pollutes air and land. Environmental education enables and encourages eco-responsibility. This is a problem we must work together to solve.

Lord God, forgive me for taking your bounteous provision for granted. Forgive me for the wastefulness of my life and help me to work with others to value every item you provide.

MICHELE D. MORRISON

Breathe on me, breath of God

The Lord God formed a man from the dust of the ground and breathed into his nostrils the breath of life, and the man became a living being. (NIV)

When my first baby, Mhairi, was born, I couldn't quite believe that this treasure was mine. I remember leaning in close, tenderly sensing her soft breath on my face. Mhairi, nurtured by me for nine months, now had her own breath to breathe, and yet, in some mysterious way, it continued to be my breath.

I grew up in Los Angeles. As new freeways allowed increased traffic to stream into the city, there were days when the APCD (Air Pollution Control District) would issue warnings that children should not play outside. Still, I played competitive tennis in school without breathing problems, but later, after living in Scotland for a few years, I attempted a game of tennis when we were visiting my parents in southern California. Within minutes, I experienced shortness of breath and pain in my chest. Breathing the fresh Scottish air for a few years had restored my lungs, perhaps, to the way God had made them. Air pollution hurt.

The ugly Covid-19 virus can be deadly when it attacks the lungs, leaving victims in agony and gasping for air. There is something deeply sinister in its targeting our breath. It is an assault on the source of life itself.

God has breathed his own life into us. How amazing is that? The Holy Spirit is often referred to as the breath of God. In Ezekiel 37, God breathes life into dry bones. The divine breath inspires and even resurrects the dead.

If we are to care for creation, we must restore the quality of the air on which we all depend. It may mean sacrificing some convenience and lifestyle comforts, but as life renews around us, it will be well worth it.

Lord, help me make choices which reduce my negative impact on this planet. May my life have a positive effect both physically and spiritually.

MICHELE D. MORRISON

The buck stops here

'Be responsible for fish in the sea and birds in the air, for every living thing that moves on the face of Earth.' Then God said, 'I've given you every sort of seed-bearing plant on Earth and every kind of fruit-bearing tree.' (MSG)

I was once given charge of a friend's goldfish while she was on holiday. I was so nervous about it going hungry that I overfed it and killed it. Taking care of creation is not easy.

Several documentaries have been made exposing brutal farming practices which condemn many animals to hellish conditions. It seems compassion dies when the 'bottom line' is our main concern. Those of us who consume, but don't farm, are not without blame, as our desire to buy food at the cheapest price is a main driver in the food production process.

There is a fear that an exploding world population requires more food than can be produced in ways that preserve a natural ecosystem. One argument for GM crops is that it increases yield to feed the world. Intensive farming methods, however, are depleting our soils of their rich diversity of minerals and nutrients. We are ravaging the earth. Yet there would be plenty of food to go around, if only we consumed and wasted less. The problem is not with the amount of food God provides; it is with unequal distribution and greed.

God has made us responsible for caring for animals and plants. How can we live ethically, and healthily, and still be able to afford food to satisfy our family's appetites? Thoughtful living is called for, requiring us to investigate the producers of what we purchase and limit ourselves to only buying what we need.

God created us in his image. We are to reflect his glory, his characteristics of compassion, kindness, goodness and love. We are called to live lives of sacrificial consideration. Even if governments are slow to act, grassroots initiatives encourage us to grow what we can, to buy seasonally and locally and to encourage a rich biodiversity that helps the ecosystem to thrive.

Lord God, break my heart for what breaks yours – may I be part of the prayerful move to bring your kingdom to earth, as it is in heaven. Give me a heart for your creation, Lord, I pray.

MICHELE D. MORRISON

It will cost us

Then the Lord said to Cain, 'Where is your brother Abel?' 'I don't know,' he replied. 'Am I my brother's keeper?' (NIV)

Why was God displeased with Cain's offering? Because it revealed his heart. Abel brought God fat portions of the firstborn of the flock. He gave God the best – not out of duty, but out of love. Cain, a farmer, brought God a gift, yes, but it was just some of the fruits of the soil. Had he brought God the juiciest cherries, the perfect pears, the plumpest tomatoes, it would have been a true sacrifice reflecting a genuine love for God.

Instead, receiving a second-rate gift, God was displeased, and that riled Cain and stirred jealousy. God warned him that he was in a dangerous place, vulnerable to sin but able to resist, but Cain did not resist. His jealousy burned. He murdered his brother and lied, flagrantly, to the Lord. His punishment? Banishment and judgement: 'When you work the ground, it will no longer yield its crops for you,' God said.

There is a mysterious connectedness between humanity and the land. When Cain lost his love for God, he lost his love for his brother. The natural consequence was a broken relationship with the rest of God's creation.

When we lose our love for God, we lose our love for our neighbours and a loss of love for creation is inevitable. The focus of our love becomes our own satisfaction. Looking out for #1 makes us disregard both our neighbours and our world. In our post-Christian world, many idols are revered, including, weirdly, the earth (Gaia). Christians don't worship the earth; we worship the creator of the earth. We love God's creation because we love him. And because we love him, we want to enjoy his creation while taking care not to spoil it. That will require some sacrifice on our part. Such sacrificial love is what God desires.

Father, we lift our eyes to the hills, not seeking help from the hills but help from the creator of the hills. May we tread lightly on this earth, leaving only a shallow footprint.

MICHELE D. MORRISON

God's rhythm to prosper

All the time that it lies desolate, the land will have the rest it did not have during the sabbaths you lived in it. (NIV)

God has put laws in place to enable creation, including humanity, to thrive. One of these laws is to observe the sabbath. God made the sabbath for man, not man for the sabbath. There is a suggestion here that the sabbath is not only for the welfare of humans, but also for the health of the land. Humans need rest. So does the land.

Intensive farming methods, developed to increase food production, deplete the soil, as we noted a few days ago. They also cruelly affect animals. Factory chickens live just over a month from egg to oven. In the US, cattle are fattened in feeding stations where they are denied grazing land. Chemicals kill pests but can poison the aquifers beneath. A landowner near us retained the well-water for his own family, thinking it superior to mains water, but after the tragedy of his wife miscarrying twins and then delivering a seriously premature baby boy, they had the well-water tested. It was lethal, full of pesticides.

Many people work 24/7. The gig economy is a relentless master. Company directors, driven by greed or fear, are never away from their phones, even on holiday. The idea of a sabbath rest, for humans or land, has been forgotten. The writer in Ecclesiastes 3 describes the beauty of the rhythm of life as God has established it, concluding 'that each of them may eat and drink, and find satisfaction in all their toil – this is the gift of God' (Ecclesiastes 3:13). God has established a rhythm by which the world will prosper, a rhythm which allows respite and rest to creatures and plant life. To ignore the rhythm is to suffer burnout, erosion, wildfires – and possibly pandemics.

I stand guilty, rarely allowing myself a sabbath day's rest. What about you? This week, make a point of taking regular breaks, lifting your eyes to the skies and praising the God who made you.

MICHELE D. MORRISON

Leading on our knees

'There is no faithfulness, no kindness, no knowledge of God in your land… That is why your land is in mourning, and everyone is wasting away. Even the wild animals, the birds of the sky, and the fish of the sea are disappearing.' (NLT)

When we lose sight of who God is and fall out of a deep personal relationship with him, we quickly stray from his principles and values. 'My people are being destroyed because they don't know me,' God complains through Hosea (v. 6).

As we have seen, a consequence of not knowing God is not caring about his creation. This is where we are in the 21st century. We need to move quickly in practical ways to stop the degradation. Coupled with this, though, we Christians should be on our knees asking forgiveness for our profligacy and selfishness, drawing deeper into relationship with God and demonstrating to others how to care for the world.

God longs for us to be faithful to him, steadfast in our love and allegiance. As we move in love for him, he will guide and enable us to live clean lives in every way, lives of restraint and magnanimity, lives of kindness and compassion. There is more healing needed than simply environmental. Our sick spirits need the healer.

I have an autoimmune disorder. I take tablets every day to protect myself from the consequences of the syndrome. The tablets don't do anything to correct the disorder, but hopefully I won't suffer any more consequences.

Many environmentalists are seeking ways to achieve zero-carbon emissions to halt global warming before the consequences bring disaster to life on this planet. There are amazing technologies being developed to remediate the damage we have already wreaked through our negligence. Perhaps world leaders will get behind this movement and we will, in fact, pull out of the environmental disaster into which we are plunging. Then what? We need greater perspective, greater understanding, and God's help, to change our natural behaviour and selfish inclinations, or we will repeat this blunder.

Father, forgive us for trashing your creation. Forgive us for neglecting our first love – you. Lead us back into close relationship with you, and may the earth rejoice, and the mountains and hills sing.

MICHELE D. MORRISON

God's megaphone

**'Who is this that darkens counsel by words without knowledge?…
Where were you when I laid the foundation of the earth?' (NRSV)**

Job's terrible misfortunes, scripture records, were a spiritual attack by the enemy. The environment emergency and the Covid-19 pandemic, on the other hand, have been caused by human behaviour, but, like Job, when we turn to God in our helplessness, he answers us.

The first thing to note is that the world we know today is not the world as God created it. In Job 38—41, God is lavish in his descriptions of the awesome world he created. His questions humble Job, and they should certainly humble us today. After vivid descriptions of the creation and some of the marvellous creatures that inhabit it, God challenges Job to explain how all of this came to be.

Job didn't have the scientific knowledge we have today, yet, although science tells us a good deal, it fails to answer the central question: who or what began it all? When we look up at the stars, when we hear of the vastness of the galaxies and the minuteness of microbes, when we crouch in a hurricane or cower in an earthquake – we have no answers.

When we break an appliance, we need the manufacturer's help to fix it. We have broken this world, and we need God's grace and mercy to help us find solutions to heal it. The church should lead in this serious struggle, humbly seeking forgiveness for our horrendous mistakes. Jesus the light shines in the darkness, and the darkness has not overcome it. We are called to be light bearers, bringing hope and leading the way to Jesus through the mess in which we are mired.

Time to silence our 'words without knowledge' and listen.

Lord God, we confess that our attitudes can be proud and self-sufficient, until we are confronted with situations beyond our knowledge. Give us listening ears, teachable spirits and willing obedience.

MICHELE D. MORRISON

A love gift

'If my people, who are called by my name, will humble themselves and pray and seek my face and turn from their wicked ways, then I will hear from heaven, and I will forgive their sin and will heal their land.' (NIV)

If you have time, read chapter 6 as well, which chronicles the exuberant, extravagant joy as Solomon led the people to God in a prayer of humble repentance and a declaration of devotion to the God of creation. The glory of God was so 'thick' in the temple that the priests couldn't even get in! The people all worshipped, first on their knees, and then with a fortnight of singing and dancing.

After such obedience and such a wonderful display of their love, God appeared to Solomon and made the above promise. Solomon had acknowledged that the people would sin again. God knew that the people would sin again. And that sin – greed, selfish ambition, thoughtless misuse of valuable resources – would impact the land.

Creation is an organic whole. The Butterfly Effect says that when a butterfly flaps its wings in New Mexico, a hurricane happens in China. We may think that our little bit – either conservation or flagrant abuse – makes no difference, but this is not true. Our actions all impact creation, for better or for worse.

Is it too late to save the planet? No. We put our trust in the God of hope, the God who promises to heal the land. But we need to repent of our flagrant abuse; we must humble ourselves and have teachable spirits and a willingness to change our lifestyles. The greater our love for God, the more natural will be our love for his creation, and out of that flows our willingness to partner with him in its stewardship.

We are in a critical time and we need inspired leaders. Pray that those whom God calls respond with courage and lead us, as Solomon led his people.

God, show me what to do. Those whom you call, you equip, and you never abandon anyone to her own strength. May we, your people, take our place partnering with you to restore life to land and seas.

MICHELE D. MORRISON

Love me, love my creation

For everything, absolutely everything, above and below, visible and invisible, rank after rank after rank of angels – *everything* **got started in him and finds its purpose in him. He… holds it all together right up to this moment. (MSG)**

Everything is held together in Jesus, who came to redeem the world (John 3:16), because he loves creation so much. I love the vibrant language of *The Message* in Colossians: 'God rescued us from dead-end alleys and dark dungeons. He's set us up in the kingdom of the Son he loves so much' (vv. 13–14).

My mom wasn't house-proud, but she kept a tidy home. She didn't have clutter on the kitchen counters. Shoes were taken off in bedrooms and kept in closets and coats were hung up. Every night, newspapers were picked up off the floor and put in the bin before bedtime. When we used to visit with our four children, I took care to maintain her standard. We were visiting her 'kingdom', and I loved her and didn't want her to find our visit overwhelming because of the mess we left everywhere.

God has set us up in the kingdom over which Jesus reigns. In this kingdom, we are responsible for our own mess. It's not just our carbon footprint. It's the greed that drives our consumer mindsets. I remember being surprised several years ago when a poll showed that a high percentage of Britons named 'shopping' as their hobby. Shopping! I once met a woman from Central America who said that in her native language, the word for 'window-shopping' was the same word as 'lust'. That is the danger of having shopping as a hobby, because the more we see, the more we want.

As we buy, we discard things we have barely worn or used. It's an abuse of all the energy and raw materials required to manufacture things; abuse of a good gift. As stewards, we should be better caretakers of the kingdom.

Lord, what I don't want to do, I do, and what I want to do, I don't do. Forgive me. My desire is to honour you by taking care of your kingdom. Help me to do my part.

MICHELE D. MORRISON

Maintain perspective

'Do not worry about your life, what you will eat or drink; or about your body, what you will wear... Look at the birds of the air; they do not sow or reap or store away in barns, and yet your heavenly Father feeds them.' (NIV)

I have a Bob Marley song in my head as I write this. In the song, three little birds advise him, 'Don't worry about a thing... every little thing is gonna be all right.' I wonder if he wrote that song after reading this passage in Matthew's gospel. Jesus is trying to shift our focus from the fear of providing for our own needs, to trusting God to provide for us.

Jesus draws our gaze to nature, changing our perspective and inviting us to meditate on the way God cares for his kingdom. Look at the birds. See the lilies. In his popular poem, 'Leisure', William Henry Davies echoed this sentiment: 'What is this life if, full of care, we have no time to stand and stare?' One blessing many people noted during the time of enforced lockdown during the Covid-19 pandemic was that, for once, they had time to stand and stare.

So much of the degradation of the earth stems from fear. When we allow ourselves to be driven by this emotion, the enemy wins. Satan seeks to ruin what God has called good. When fear trumps faith, peace is shattered, and our attention is on caring for ourselves rather than caring for the world that God gave us.

Fear of insufficiency makes us grabby and grippy. As we focus on ourselves, we develop wasteful habits. A fortnight after the first wave of panic-buying during the Covid-19 pandemic, refuse collectors emptied bins overflowing with rotting fruits and vegetables, discarded without ever having been unwrapped. It's a microcosm of business-as-usual globally, where the 'developed' world hoards and wastes, while the rest of the world suffers deprivation.

Seek first the kingdom of God. Only buy clothes when you need them. Don't buy more food than you and your family can consume. Don't build up treasures on earth; focus on God.

MICHELE D. MORRISON

You can make a difference

Against its will, all creation was subjected to God's curse. But with eager hope, the creation looks forward to the day when it will join God's children in glorious freedom from death and decay. (NLT)

When Adam and Eve surrendered to temptation in the garden, they dragged all creation out of God's favour. The natural world became collateral damage of the fall. Humanity's focus had slipped from God to self, and stewardship of the natural world now correlated to a seeking after personal enhancement of worldly pleasures and power rather than glorification of God.

The writer to the Romans gives creation itself a personality and an ambition: a yearning to return to the harmony and shalom of the garden of Eden, an eager hope for release from bondage, death and decay. All creation eagerly awaits the revelation of who God's children really are.

How will that happen? How will God's children be revealed? Not by what we say, but by who we are, because this affects what we do. As God's children, we have his attributes, his love, his delight, his kindness, his selflessness. The Spirit, living in us, develops these 'fruits' in us, and it is these attributes which will impact the world. We can no longer be party to the wanton destruction of planet earth. Our hard hearts are softened and broken by what breaks the heart of God: cruelty to wildlife, selfish exploitation of resources and careless consumption which costs the earth dear.

This rings true in all believers. We long for release from sin. Jesus has saved us, and when we accept that we can't save ourselves, we humbly recognise that we don't know where to begin to restore the environment. I remember the story of the little boy horrified by the sight of a carpet of starfish stranded on a beach. As he threw them back into the sea, one by one, a cynic pointed out the futility of his action. He threw another one in and responded: 'It made a difference to that starfish.'

We can all make a difference. 'The Holy Spirit helps us in our weakness.' As we allow him to help us, we are revealed as children of God. Spend time listening for the Spirit's guidance now.

MICHELE D. MORRISON

Praise our creator!

He set the earth on its foundations; it can never be moved. (NIV)

This psalm celebrates in poetic beauty the intimate involvement of our mighty God in every detail of his world. We humans are powerless in the face of hurricane, earthquake, storm and pestilence. We are dependent on nature delivering a pleasant climate, adequate rainfall, warm sunshine, and this psalm reminds us of just who controls nature. 'How many are your works, Lord! In wisdom you made them all' (v. 24).

Christians are characterised by the hope they have in the creator God, who set the earth on its foundations and promises it can never be moved. Psalm 24, with which we started these devotions, states that the world was founded on the seas. As we saw in Colossians, 'in [Jesus] all things hold together' (1:17). Jesus is the earth's foundation.

When I was two, my parents gave me a pull-along toy lamb which bleated as she moved. I loved that lamb, and eagerly fed her bits of paper. Eventually she was so full of paper, she could no longer baa. I had mistreated my parents' gift and broken it. They couldn't fix it, but neither did they punish me for spoiling the toy. I'd broken it out of ignorance.

God forgives and restores. He who makes grass grow for the cattle on a thousand hills can indeed make the lamb bleat once more. As we renew our relationship with him, loving him with all our heart, soul, mind and strength, and loving our neighbours as ourselves, then our relationship with the earth will be healed. Let's celebrate God's creation, which he loves. One day Jesus will return, and heaven will come to earth forever. We do not fear annihilation; again, we need not panic.

(Based on verses from Psalm 104.) May the glory of the Lord endure forever; may the Lord rejoice in his works. May my meditation be pleasing to him, as I rejoice in the Lord. Praise the Lord, O my soul. Praise the Lord.

MICHELE D. MORRISON

Habakkuk: prophet of hope

Amy Boucher Pye writes:

Are you sitting comfortably? We're about to embark on a fortnight with an often-overlooked prophet from the Old Testament, Habakkuk. Sometimes his conversation with God will sting, so you might wonder why I call him a prophet of hope. Hearing what God says he's going to do to his people makes Habakkuk quiver, weep and lament. But as we will see, even though he tries to bargain with God, yet he trusts in him. In the end, he holds out hope.

So I have to warn you that we'll face some difficult passages to explore from this minor prophet. And yet, for those who experience disappointment, heartbreak and pain – which of course is all of us – we can find comfort and hope from one of God's people who voiced his feelings to God. Through Habakkuk's conversation with God, his outlook changes.

By the time we reach the book of Habakkuk, God's people have enjoyed some glory days under King David and his son Solomon but are now in decline. Under Solomon's son, the kingdom splits into two, into the northern tribe of Israel and the southern of Judah. The Assyrian people to the west conquer Israel, taking the Israelites hostage, and soon the same fate will befall the people of Judah when the Babylonians seek domination. Habakkuk is God's messenger of the woes to come.

Thus, the American pastor Charles Swindoll has said of the book of Habakkuk that it's made up of 'two sobs and a song'. This is an apt description, for the book is made up of two of Habakkuk's laments and God's replies, and then the song of Habakkuk in response. He is the minor prophet who speaks directly with God instead of delivering a message to the people from God.

We will find parts of this book challenging and hard, but I hope you'll also see how God's love underpins his concern for his people. Although he is a holy God who demands justice, yet he shows mercy too. May you experience that love and mercy as you read and ponder these conversations and the song of praise to the living Lord.

I'm grateful for the help in understanding this prophet from various commentaries and books, but especially the NIV Application Commentary *Habakkuk* by James Bruckner (Zondervan, 2004).

Why, Lord?

The prophecy that Habakkuk the prophet received. How long, Lord, must I call for help, but you do not listen? Or cry out to you, 'Violence!' but you do not save? Why do you make me look at injustice? Why do you tolerate wrongdoing? (NIV)

Reading the book of Habakkuk during the coronavirus pandemic resonates as I ponder the question, 'Why?' Why are so many people around the world stricken with this disease? Why do so many suffer? As I consider the horrific thought of people dying alone, I wonder if their relatives feel like this prophet when he says to God, 'You're not listening!'

This short Old Testament book doesn't outline God's comprehensive answers to the question of why. But it illustrates how we can handle these deep concerns, for like the prophet we can pour them out to the Lord. We see this principle embedded in the very first sentence, which we might be tempted to glance over as an introductory statement. Yet knowing that the prophecy – or 'oracle', which in the original Hebrew implies 'burden' – was given to Habakkuk by God underlines that our creator expects us to lament. He welcomes us to bring our griefs to him.

Habakkuk doesn't hold back in his cries as he says not only 'How long?' but 'Why?' He wonders why, if Yahweh is a good God, can he tolerate all this wrongdoing, destruction, violence and conflict? Why do evildoers pervert the cause of justice?

As we'll see tomorrow, God doesn't always answer as we would expect. But we can trust that he is a faithful God who groans with us over all that is wrong with the world. He doesn't silence our cries but welcomes us to voice them to him. He hears our laments and doesn't dismiss our pain, anxiety or fears. As we come to him, we can find hope, peace and love – even amid the crises we live through.

Loving Lord, thank you for letting us express every feeling we have to you, and especially those of lament. Hear my cries and my fears and be with me; give me the peace of your presence.

AMY BOUCHER PYE

Unbelievable

'Look at the nations and watch – and be utterly amazed. For I am going to do something in your days that you would not believe, even if you were told.' (NIV)

One of my favourite spiritual companions is the 16th-century Spaniard, Teresa of Avila. She's witty and smart, and I love her passion for God. Once when travelling to a group of cloistered women for whom she had over-sight, she fell off her horse into a cold stream. Complaining to God, her immediate retort was, 'Dear Lord, if this is how you treat your friends, it is no wonder you have so few!'

I wonder if Habakkuk felt the same when he heard God's response to his questions. For the Lord says to him, in effect, 'You're going to be absolutely blown away by what I'm going to do. You wouldn't believe it even if you could see it! I'm going to raise up and empower your deepest enemies, those cruel people who take land that isn't their own. Watch and see!'

God's answer wasn't what Habakkuk was looking for. The Lord was doing something much bigger than Habakkuk then understood – God was going to use Judah's enemies to halt the wayward ways of his people. God had deeper purposes at work as well, which were revealed when the apostle Paul quoted from Habakkuk when teaching with Barnabas in the synagogue. Paul urged those there to believe in Jesus as the Messiah, saying, 'Look, you scoffers, wonder and perish, for I am going to do something… that you would never believe' (Acts 13:41).

When we get frustrated with how we perceive God is acting – or not – we can remember that he is God and we are not. He might be doing something much bigger than we could imagine, or other forces may be at play. In times of fog and uncertainty, we can trust that God will eventually clear the mist and that we again will enjoy his sunshine.

'Now to him who is able to do immeasurably more than all we ask or imagine, according to his power that is at work within us, to him be glory in the church and in Christ Jesus!' (Ephesians 3:20–21).

AMY BOUCHER PYE

A law unto themselves

'They mock kings and scoff at rulers. They laugh at all fortified cities; by building earthen ramps they capture them. Then they sweep past like the wind and go on – guilty people, whose own strength is their god.' (NIV)

God's prophets retain their individuality while they deliver their message, each keeping their own style – including Habakkuk. Notice how Habakkuk's personality comes through in his prophecy through his vibrant language, even when the subject matter is dire, as we see today.

Some biblical commentators think that Habakkuk belongs to the tribe of Levi, those who led the worship in the temple and the only ones who could use musical instruments to do so. His name means 'embrace' or 'to cling', such as keeping warm through physical contact. As he cries out to God, he stays close to the Lord. Even in his increasing bewilderment over God promoting the enemies of his people, Habakkuk never turns away from him.

God acknowledges that the Babylonians are a 'dreaded people' who are 'a law to themselves' (v. 7). The ruthlessness and speed of animals illustrates their character – they are fiercer than wolves at nightfall and they fly like an eagle who swoops to devour (v. 8). They resemble an all-encompassing desert wind that sweeps up everything in their midst (v. 9). They will render a city's defences useless by piling up rubble to make a ramp so that they can climb over those tall walls as they mock the formerly strong rulers (v. 10).

Note especially the final sentence from God's response: that for the Babylonians, 'strength is their god' (v. 11). Although the Lord will use these ruthless people to bring judgement against his own people, he recognises that they will not follow him. He will not save them as he will save his own people.

When we face storms that envelop us, yet we can cling to God, the one who saves us.

Loving creator, you formed us to love and serve you. Help me to put aside all that distracts me from this, my main purpose, and show me what it means to live my life for your glory.

AMY BOUCHER PYE

God our rock

Lord, are you not from everlasting? My God, my Holy One, you will never die… You, my Rock, have ordained them to punish. Your eyes are too pure to look on evil; you cannot tolerate wrongdoing. Why then do you tolerate the treacherous? (NIV)

Why, Lord? Why did my loved one suffer a heart attack? Why did my neighbour get cancer? Why does my brother have epilepsy? Why did those girls bully my child? Why did my husband get bullied? Why did my friend die so young? Why did my friend's child die? Why could something so ordinary as a peanut harm my child? Why?

It didn't take me long to roll off those questions to God. I suspect you could reel off your own list of lament and complaint, of questions asking, 'Why?' But when we follow Habakkuk's ways, we add a necessary antidote: Lord, you are good. You are holy and you love me. You're my rock and my redeemer; you will never die. I may not understand why all that stuff happens, but I know that you are with me.

As we turn to Habakkuk's second cry of complaint, notice how he sets his case before God while affirming God's qualities. 'Are you not from everlasting?' he asks (v. 12). You are holy; you're a rock; you're too pure to look on evil. He reminds himself (and God's people) of God's characteristics, knowing that a just God has ways beyond what he may understand immediately.

Even though Habakkuk grapples with the pain that is to come through the Babylonians, he puts his hope in God. Soon their enemies will capture the Hebrews and banish them from Judah, the southern kingdom. They will live in exile, away from the promised land. Yet Habakkuk looks to God, the one he knows who will never die.

When we face dire problems and what seem to be hopeless situations, we can cry out to God with our questions while we remind him and ourselves of who he is.

Comforting Spirit, quell my anxieties and fear as I remind myself of your love and care. May I immerse myself in your truth. You are the everlasting God who will never leave me.

AMY BOUCHER PYE

Hooks and nets

You have made people like the fish in the sea, like the sea creatures that have no ruler. The wicked foe pulls all of them up with hooks, he catches them in his net, he gathers them up in his drag-net; and so he rejoices and is glad. (NIV)

We might think of fishing as a genial pastime – the shimmering lake or sea, the peaceful moments, the feeling of being suspended above a body of water. But when we think of it from the point of view of the fish, the picture rather changes! Or indeed, as Habakkuk considered, when the foe of God's people snares them with hooks and nets.

How familiar are you with these opponents of God's people, the Babylonians? They had wrested control of the promised land from the Assyrians by defeating them and taking over their capital, Nineveh, in the eighth and seventh centuries BC. They then set their sights on Judah, which is what God warns Habakkuk about. Indeed, they attacked in 605, 597 and 586BC. Biblical scholars thus believe that Habakkuk wrote his book sometime in the years before the first attack in 605BC.

Habakkuk notes that their foe delights in defeating their opponents, even bowing down in worship to the tools of their warfare. We see this in verse 16: 'Therefore he sacrifices to his net and burns incense to his drag-net.' How, Habakkuk asks, can the Lord tolerate such idolatry? Will the enemy keep on 'destroying nations without mercy' (v. 17)?

We might have a different enemy from that of a marauding nation, but we shouldn't forget the influence in our lives of Satan, God's opponent. God is stronger and more powerful than the evil one, but Satan can yet affect us through his evil schemes. We, like Habakkuk, can cry out to our creator. As we put our trust in God and look to him for protection and help, he will save us from the snares and traps set before us.

Lord Jesus Christ, you suffered betrayal, gossip, persecution and ultimately death. You know what it is like to have a wicked opponent. Shield us from the schemes of the evil one, that we might bring glory to your Father.

AMY BOUCHER PYE

Those who wait

'For the revelation awaits an appointed time; it speaks of the end and will not prove false. Though it linger, wait for it; it will certainly come and will not delay.' (NIV)

'Good things come to those who wait.' We might utter this adage unthinkingly to a friend who yearns for a husband, a baby, a job or news of their loved one. We may not, however, consider that in our fallen world the things that come to those who wait can be bad, not good – or somewhere in between. The saying is true if we look through the lens of eternity, for those who follow Jesus will find all good things when we are united with God in his kingdom in heaven. But here on earth, we often experience some good, and some not so good, things.

Habakkuk, now that he has presented God with his two complaints, places himself at the city walls to watch and wait. God's answer will include the welcome news that the oppressors of God's people will themselves face ruin. But the Hebrews will still have to face exile from the land, meaning the lack of a home.

God is keen that Habakkuk understands that what he says needs to be noted and shared with the people. He tells the prophet to write down what he's going to say 'and make it plain on tablets' (v. 2). These tablets would have been visible in the same way that billboards are today.

But God's people will have to exercise faith as they wait for these words to come true. The Lord reassures Habakkuk that his words are worth waiting for: 'Though it linger [or the more poetic but old-fashioned 'tarry'], wait for it' (v. 3). He and the people may lose heart as the years pass, but in the right time – without delay – the revelation will not prove false (v. 3).

We all wait. Can we trust God while doing so?

Father God, you waited for the right time to send your Son to live among us. One day, Lord Jesus, you will come again. As we wait, strengthen our resolve to place our hope and trust in you.

AMY BOUCHER PYE

By faith

'See, the enemy is puffed up; his desires are not upright – but the righteous person will live by his faithfulness.' (NIV)

Some say that Habakkuk 2:4 is responsible for the Protestant Reformation. Martin Luther, then a monk, had travelled to Rome to take part in a religious practice in order to seek the rewards then offered by the Pope. When doing so, a flash of this verse came to mind: 'the just shall live by his faith' (KJV). He stopped what he was doing, journeyed home to Germany and started to work out a different way of understanding God and humanity to the excesses of that day.

The righteous person living by God's faithfulness is contrasted here with the enemy, which in this context describes the Babylonians. They are puffed up by too much wine, given to pride and arrogance. That, combined with their insatiable greed, moves them to gather up as many nations and peoples as they can, along with the stuff they've accumulated through stealing and extortion. But we can see a hint of God's coming judgement on them in the words, 'he is as greedy as the grave' (v. 5). The oppressors of God's people will one day meet their maker and face the consequences of their sins and destruction.

Knowing that all will be well in the end gives us strength and hope, but that doesn't mean we won't struggle before then when we witness evil seemingly win. We may be tempted to lose hope or to despair. If so, we can ask God to give us his perspective. We can seek him for an infusion of hope and the strength to keep on following and serving him. He delights to answer these prayers and will give us what we need for that day.

Lord, how difficult we find it when those who stand against us succeed. Help us to lean on you in all things. Help us too to let go of the things that entangle us or keep us from you.

AMY BOUCHER PYE

Statements of woe

'Because you have plundered many nations, the peoples who are left will plunder you. For you have shed human blood; you have destroyed lands and cities and everyone in them.' (NIV)

Many Christians find parts of the Old Testament difficult. Why the wrath? Why the exercise of judgement? Well-loved Bible teacher J.I. Packer addresses the question in *Knowing God*: 'God's wrath in the Bible is never the capricious, self-indulgent, irritable, morally ignoble thing that human anger so often is. It is, instead, a right and necessary reaction to objective moral evil.'

The God of the Old Testament has the same character as the God of the New Testament – loving but also just. When we think about God's judgement, we can hold it within the overarching story of scripture, of God's love for his people and how he sent his own Son to die as the sacrifice for sin. We know too of God's unending love for his people.

This part of Habakkuk's conversation with God can feel difficult to follow, for the words seem to jut here and there. As God responds to Habakkuk's complaints, he outlines what will happen to Judah's foes through five statements of 'woe'. Bible scholars note that these woes are meant to be ironic – as the NRSV says, 'Alas' instead of 'Woe'. God empowers those who are oppressed with the task of speaking out these statements of impending judgement. Their words will form a lament spoken against those who torment them.

The first statement is woe to them who become wealthy through stealing from others, for those who prey upon others will be preyed upon (vv. 6–7). They will face ruin (v. 8). The oppressors' reign of destruction will end.

As we think about evil and judgement, we can take heart that good will triumph in the end.

'What a wretched man I am! Who will rescue me from this body that is subject to death? Thanks be to God, who delivers me through Jesus Christ our Lord!' (Romans 7:24–25).

AMY BOUCHER PYE

More woes

**'For the earth will be filled with the knowledge of the glory of
the Lord as the waters cover the sea.' (NIV)**

One of my favourite picture books when I was a child was called *The Rich
Fool*, based on Jesus' parable in Luke 12:16–21. I can see in my mind's eye
the bright colours on the cover and the image of the man who had more
grain than he knew what to do with. The story captured my imagination –
how this man built more and more silos to hold the grain and went to bed
satisfied, not knowing that he'd just lived his last day on the earth.

Jesus' story resonates with the second warning to the enemy that
Habakkuk receives from the Lord. Woe to those who build their houses –
with the meaning of the word in Hebrew including a sense of a dynasty –
through wicked ways, for they will face ruin. The image-rich language
shares how the very stones used in the structure will cry out against the
injustice (v. 11).

The third woe concerns those who gain their power and riches through
violence and injustice. They, God says, will exhaust themselves for nothing (v. 13). Notice verse 14, which marks roughly halfway through the five
woes, and how it breaks up the words of judgement: God's glory will shine
forth in the earth. He will not be shaken by the enemies of the Judeans.

How do you think God's people felt when they read Habakkuk's revelation of these woes to come for their enemies? Although they knew they
would be banished from their home, they could find assurance in the
promises of God that he'd never desert them – and that those whom he
sent to judge them would themselves be judged.

For us, too, God will make everything right.

---

*Father God, when I see or experience injustice, help me to give my com-
plicated feelings to you as I pray about the matter. You are a loving and
fair judge.*

AMY BOUCHER PYE

Yet more woes

'Woe to him who says to wood, "Come to life!" Or to lifeless stone, "Wake up!" Can it give guidance? It is covered with gold and silver; there is no breath in it. The Lord is in his holy temple; let all the earth be silent before him.' (NIV)

We might be tempted to believe that the world has never been more depraved than it is now, when we hear of crimes and acts of violence or aggression. But evil and turning from God are nothing new, as we see in the fourth and fifth woes that God tells Habakkuk to document.

The fourth is particularly shocking as it concerns wanton debauchery, assault and pillage. The Babylonians would get their victims drunk before assaulting them, but God warns that he will wrap these oppressors in disgrace. Indeed, he will reveal their nakedness, which in the Hebrew is even more shocking than what we read in English, for the original language implies the uncovering of a man's foreskin. Those who torture others will be exposed.

The Babylonians hurt not only people but also the animals and the land, as we see in verse 17. Their destruction knows no bounds as they decimate land, cities, people and animals. God will not allow this to continue.

The fifth woe concerns the breaking of the first commandment, not to have any other gods before Yahweh (Exodus 20:3). The Babylonians worship not the true and living God, but an idol 'that cannot speak' – something of their own creation (v. 18). Idols made of wood and stone will never wake up and guide the people; they should look to the Lord in his holy temple (v. 20).

After three days of wading through these woes, we can exhale in relief, for we've reached the end of them. Perhaps our best response is similar to what we'll see tomorrow – Habakkuk turns to prayer. We can pray for the persecuted and ask God to reveal in us any hardness of heart that would lead us away from him.

'Though outwardly we are wasting away, yet inwardly we are being renewed day by day. For our light and momentary troubles are achieving for us an eternal glory that far outweighs them all' (2 Corinthians 4:16–17).

AMY BOUCHER PYE

Remember mercy

Lord, I have heard of your fame; I stand in awe of your deeds, Lord. Repeat them in our day, in our time make them known; in wrath remember mercy. (NIV)

Do you want the good news or the not-so-good news? The good news is that we've left the woes and have reached Habakkuk's prayer, which is a song of three stanzas and a refrain. The not-so-good news? Habakkuk remains terrified of the judgement to come. For it will come.

Habakkuk has moved through the stages of grief – from denial and anger in his questions of 'Why?' in chapter 1 to bargaining, depression and more denial. Finally, he moves in this song to a form of acceptance. He may not understand God's actions, but he will trust in him.

Habakkuk starts the song off by affirming the character and action of God, saying that he stands in awe of him (v. 2). Then we see the first of what is called a theophany – of God appearing to humanity in physical form. God comes to a special place, the region of Mount Sinai, and appears in splendorous light, shaking the earth with his power (vv. 3–6). Habakkuk's song reflects his awareness of his own smallness compared with the might and majesty of the Lord. He is awed and humbled even as he asks, at the beginning of the song, for God to repeat his good deeds. Even as Habakkuk trembles at the sight of God, he yet seeks relief for his people: 'in wrath remember mercy' (v. 2).

I wonder if we focus enough on the power and might of God today. Jesus surely is our friend and our brother, but because of the intimacy we receive through him and the Spirit, we might be tempted to forget the holiness and majesty of the Father who created us. Why not ask God to increase your awe of him, so that you can worship him for his power and might?

Heavenly Father, you are holy and good. You are pure and mighty. I know that you seek a pure and undefiled heart; create in me a clean heart so that I might bring honour to you.

AMY BOUCHER PYE

All-powerful God

In wrath you strode through the earth and in anger you threshed the nations. You came out to deliver your people, to save your anointed one. (NIV)

As I mentioned earlier, I am writing in the midst of the lockdown during the coronavirus pandemic. Realising just how quickly our day-to-day activities can change amid this silent killer reminds me that I'm not at the centre of the universe. Reading James Bruckner's NIV Application Commentary *Habakkuk* brought this thought home, in a line that feels apposite: 'The dramatic manifestations of shattering mountains and devastating plagues serve the creator in decimating the view that the creation is centered on humanity.'

I certainly don't think God has caused this pandemic, and I know he's weeping at the losses and griefs so many are suffering. But I also believe he is using these times for the strengthening of his people and his name. That the world could shut down so quickly reminds us of our smallness and our vulnerabilities. We, like Habakkuk, can turn to God in prayer as we ask him for help.

In the second and third stanzas of his song, Habakkuk shares more theophanies of God appearing in his might and power. Here is the creator-warrior, he who shaped the earth with rivers and mountains, and who flashes through the skies with his spear of lightning. We see hints of God's cosmic purposes to come through his Son Jesus: 'You came out to deliver your people, to save your anointed one' (v. 13). But God will also crush the wicked, which will impact Habakkuk and his people.

Take some time today to ponder the many images in verses 9–15. Which of them stand out to you most, and why? How do you respond to thinking about God in this way as a creator-warrior? Why?

'But ask the animals, and they will teach you, or the birds in the sky, and they will tell you… In his hand is the life of every creature and the breath of all mankind' (Job 12:7, 10).

AMY BOUCHER PYE

Rejoicing during trials

Though the fig-tree does not bud and there are no grapes on the vines, though the olive crop fails and the fields produce no food… yet I will rejoice in the Lord, I will be joyful in God my Saviour. (NIV)

Stress can manifest in our bodies, and Habakkuk's response to his terror over the coming calamities reveals itself bodily: 'my heart pounded, my lips quivered… my legs trembled' (v. 16). Although he shakes in fear, yet he will trust in God, waiting for the coming of what God has promised to do through the marauding oppressors. In this he responds to God's earlier direction to wait, as we saw last week in Habakkuk 2:3 ('though it linger, wait for it').

Habakkuk is aware of the food shortages to come. There will be no figs or olives, no sheep or cattle. Although he and God's people face starvation, yet he affirms his trust in God: 'yet I will rejoice in the Lord, I will be joyful in God my Saviour' (v. 18).

For those of us who live in a developed country, we can hardly fathom what these kind of food shortages would look like. After the panic-buying of the early days of the pandemic, we faced supermarkets with bare shelves. But each morning they were restocked – we were never in danger of going hungry. But of course, life in the ancient Near East was vastly different, and they would face starvation. How amazing that Habakkuk, though trembling, yet promises to rejoice in the God who saves him. Not only will he live and survive, but he'll thrive.

Whatever crisis we face, and however much we quiver, yet we can put all our faith and trust in the God who hears us, loves us, redeems us and will never leave us. His word is true. May we look to him for our strength and our hope.

'The Lord reigns, let the nations tremble; he sits enthroned between the cherubim, let the earth shake… Let them praise your great and awesome name – he is holy' (Psalm 99:1, 3).

AMY BOUCHER PYE

Standing on the rock

The Sovereign Lord is my strength; he makes my feet like the feet of a deer, he enables me to tread on the heights. (NIV)

Many people, when thinking of Habakkuk, might call to mind the allegorical novel *Hinds' Feet on High Places* by Hannah Hurnard. In it, the main character, Much Afraid, journeys through many travails to become a mature disciple of Christ. She longs to have the feet of a deer who can walk safely in the treacherous high places – which comes from the last line of Habakkuk's song.

The ending of this song is perhaps the most encouraging part of Habakkuk's prophecy, and all the more so because of the forthcoming anguish and woes that he outlines. Habakkuk knows what is to come – bloodshed, poverty, destruction – but he finds his strength in the sovereign Lord. The circumstances haven't changed, but he trusts that with God's power he will navigate the cliffs without falling.

His choice of a deer scampering over the high places fits well with verse 18, in which he affirms that he will trust God joyfully. In their grace and beauty as they move, deer seem to convey a joyful approach to life.

As we look back over the past fortnight of engaging with a sometimes-overlooked minor prophet, let's remember how he models holding a conversation with God – he presents his complaints and requests but also accepts the word of the sovereign Lord.

Let us consider the effects of turning from God and sin, and how whole nations and people groups can be affected by the evil deeds of some. We can remind ourselves of our smallness as God's created individuals, trusting that he as our creator loves us and cares for the big and small things that concern us. And we, with Habakkuk, can proclaim that we will tread on the heights with the feet of the deer, for the Lord is our strength.

Lord, you are our strength and our song! When we face trials, we know that you are with us, guiding us and upholding us. Give us the feet of a deer to stand in the high places!

AMY BOUCHER PYE

In God's eyes

Tracy Williamson writes:

When I received the email asking if I would like to write a series looking at some of the ways God describes us, my heart gave a little leap, as this theme is dear to me. Over my three decades as a Christian, God has brought deep healing into my life through my growing understanding of how he sees me, what he says about me and the trust he puts in me to do his works.

My journey began one day when I was reading Matthew 3, the story of Jesus' baptism. As I read the Father's words about Jesus: 'This is my dearly loved Son, who brings me great joy' (Matthew 3:17, NLT), shivers went up my spine. I felt the Holy Spirit with me, as if he was highlighting those words and saying in my heart: 'As Jesus was my dearly loved Son, so too are you my beloved daughter. As Jesus brings me great joy, so too do you bring me joy. You are my beloved.'

At first, I could hardly believe this was God. I had been told so often that I was rubbish, a mistake, stupid. I lived in shame, always hiding my face and afraid to speak. I wanted my life to count, but I believed I should never have been born. Becoming a Christian had opened my heart to hope, and I now knew in my head that God loved me, but I still struggled with so many lies.

What God said to me that day was the beginning of a growing understanding of how precious I am to him. I began to find truth after truth in his word: that he had always intended me to be his child; that I am beautiful to him; totally forgiven and pure in his eyes; uniquely created; an ambassador of his love; gifted; chosen and anointed… With the help of Christian friends I learnt to renounce the old negatives and pray that God would help me receive and live out the truth. I am still on that journey today.

I pray that as you reflect upon these beautiful truths of who you are in God's eyes, you will know the joy of his love in a deeper way than ever before. Listen for his voice and write down all he shows you as you journey through the series.

You are his beloved, the apple of his eye.

Planned from the beginning

For he chose us in him before the creation of the world to be holy and blameless in his sight. In love he predestined us for adoption to sonship through Jesus Christ. (NIV)

As we consider how God sees us, I love these verses showing that even before he created this universe, God planned for us to belong to him as his dearly loved children.

Are you a planner? Personally, I am more of a drifter and often run away from the need to get ready or organise my time. Yet when I do take the time to prepare, I feel a deep joy in envisaging, as it were, the finished blog or book and the people whose lives may be touched as a result.

Here we see that from the very beginning God felt that same joy in planning for us to become his children, children who are holy and blameless in his sight. How amazing! I so easily fall into condemnation, dredging up all the ways I feel I don't match up to others who seem so much holier. Maybe you feel like that too. In fact, I have a deep sense that for someone reading this, you constantly struggle with self-hatred. You've experienced the pain of hearing so many negative words that you just cannot believe that God or anyone else could love you and want you with them. Maybe you grew up hearing that you were a mistake.

I know what that pain feels like, but as I've grown in my experience of God's love, I've come to understand how deeply God feels that pain too. The truth is we have always been planned and wanted. He created you with joy, anticipating your uniqueness and the ways he would use you to reflect his beauty. He sent his precious Son to die so that there would be nothing that could stop us belonging to him.

May you know today the wonder of always having been planned and wanted.

Spend time rereading this passage. Remember God is with you and loves you. Give him all your negative feelings and ask him to free you to know the truth that you were planned and wanted from the very beginning.

TRACY WILLIAMSON

Beloved child

'But while he was still a long way off, his father saw him and was filled with compassion for him; he ran to his son, threw his arms round him and kissed him.' (NIV)

Jesus longed for people to understand his Father's passionate love for them. They knew God as Lord but not as dad. Jesus was using a shock strategy here, because it was unheard of for a son to demand his inheritance – literally wishing his father dead! His disrespect was through the roof and people would expect the father to disown him.

Maybe you feel that you too have so messed up that God could never love you. But that is a lie. Jesus told this story so that you could experience the Father's kiss of love and know you are his beloved child. John says: 'See what great love the Father has lavished on us, that we should be called children of God! And that is what we are!' (1 John 3:1).

Another shock would have been Jesus' description of the father's uninhibited response to his son's return. He should have been cold and constrained! I wonder how often we act in constrained ways, appearing to be the perfect Christian, when really God feels a million miles away? The elder son was like that, slaving for his father, who had already given him everything. He was miserable and jealous, yet his father clearly loved him.

We all express aspects of both son's mindsets, but Jesus wants us to see the Father's love for us. He ran to his son. Do you know he runs to you too? He kissed him and dignified him by giving him a fine robe and a ring, denoting he was his heir as well as his son. And then he threw a party for him.

The older son is not forgotten either, as the father goes to see him and assures him of his love.

Whatever we have done or whatever lies we have believed, God says, 'You are my beloved child.' Will we live in that joy?

Ask your heavenly Father to speak to you as you reflectively read this story again. Can you see elements of both sons in your own thinking? Imagine Father God running to lavish his love on you. How will you respond?

TRACY WILLIAMSON

Chosen friend

'I no longer call you servants, because a servant does not know his master's business. Instead, I have called you friends, for everything that I learned from my Father I have made known to you. You did not choose me, but I chose you.' (NIV)

Today's passage is amazing because its whole message is about being chosen. Jesus is saying that he wants a relationship with you above everything else. He told his disciples: 'I chose you. I picked you to be my friends and, out of that relationship, for you to do wonderful things with me.' His desire for them was to be close, to understand that he delighted in being with them and sharing his 'family' secrets.

We tell our friends things that we may never tell our family. I was given a mug once that said, 'Friends are the family we choose for ourselves.' You can be yourself with your friend. You don't have to mind your p's and q's. You can tell them if you are struggling and know they will care or celebrate if you've had good news. Marilyn is such a friend to me. We laugh or cry together, and she does her utmost to help me when I can't hear. We communicate.

Jesus says that his gift of friendship is based on communication. Do you expect to hear Jesus? The other week I was panicking about meeting a deadline and a clear thought came to me: 'Rest in me. You can do it.' Jesus was speaking as a friend. He knew my focus was on the deadline, but it needed to be on him. He knew I could do it if I just rested in his love. Out of that word of friendship came the fruit of a beautiful piece of writing.

Jesus says, 'Remain in my love.' Let's believe what he says about us: 'As the Father has loved me, so have I loved you'. He couldn't be more direct: 'My Father and I are so close and that's what I want with you, my chosen friend.'

Think of somewhere relaxing, maybe your garden or a favourite sofa. Picture Jesus there, excited about spending time with you. Sit together and imagine smiling at each other. What do you want to tell him? What will he tell you?

TRACY WILLIAMSON

You are beautiful

My beloved spoke and said to me, 'Arise, my darling, my beautiful one, come with me. See! The winter is past; the rains are over and gone. Flowers appear on the earth; the season of singing has come.' (NIV)

God is calling to you, 'You are my beautiful one. I love you; I delight in you; you reveal the glory of my Son. You are my bride.'

How do those words make you feel? Throughout my childhood I constantly heard that I was ugly and stupid, so it seems incredible that God calls me 'beautiful one'. Yet these words are not just about Solomon's love for a woman, but also about God's passionate love for us, his bride. In 4:7 he says, 'You are altogether beautiful, my darling; there is no flaw in you.'

Of course, we do have flaws, and sometimes they are all we can think of: 'I'm too fat!' or 'I've messed up again.' We are so aware of our failings, so how can God describe us as flawless?

Remember that Jesus willingly took all the ugliness in our lives and gave us his own purity instead. We have the true beauty of his life and love within us instead of the ashes of our brokenness (Isaiah 61:3). This is the beauty of his love, compassion, gentleness and kindness being made real in our lives.

Our sense of shame makes us hide, but God constantly calls us out of hiding: 'My dove… show me your face, let me hear your voice.' He never gives up calling us to come and be with him. He says, 'The winter is past; the rains are over and gone.' The winter and rains are symbolic of all the negatives the devil has used to cripple us, but Jesus carried them on to the cross so that we could be free. He calls us today to enter the springtime of knowing we are loved and beautiful because of him.

Please believe that you are his beautiful one whose face he longs to see and whose voice he longs to hear.

Lord Jesus, thank you that you took my ugliness so I could become beautiful. I respond today to your call to leave the winter behind and come into the spring, to come out of hiding into the intimacy of your love. Amen
TRACY WILLIAMSON

Empowered to know his thoughts

What we have received is not the spirit of the world, but the Spirit who is from God, so that we may understand what God has freely given us. This is what we speak, not in words taught us by human wisdom but in words taught by the Spirit. (NIV)

God has done everything to enable us to draw close to him. This passage is so encouraging because it shows clearly that God loves us to know his thoughts and be part of what he is doing. He gives us his own Spirit to communicate God's words to us.

This is especially meaningful to me as a deaf person. I cannot hear what anyone says unless someone types or writes their words out for me because reading is my preferred way of understanding. Other deaf people may prefer to lip-read or use BSL (British Sign Language). In the same way, we each hear God in our own unique way. What does that look like for you?

I often find that something ordinary becomes significant and as I reflect upon it, God then speaks into my heart. For example, my hearing dog Goldie loves to jump fences. Today, when he did that, I sensed God wanted me to reflect on how Goldie's love of exploring overrides any sense of containment. God said, 'I want you to dare to explore things that interest you; to not be bound by others' opinions.' That was exciting!

A Bible verse or a Christian song may 'grab' you in a similar way, or it may be an idea or a nudging to do something. You may have a picture or a vision, or hear words in your mind that you know are not your natural thoughts. The key is to reflect and talk to God about what it might mean. Have a journal to hand. You may be amazed at the insights that come.

I believe someone reading this note has always felt excluded when others are talking or planning things. God wants to heal this wound. He loves you and loves speaking with you. Open your heart to his voice today.

Father, thank you for the gift of your Spirit and that because you made me, you know how best to reach me. Forgive me for my lack of faith. I choose to listen for your voice of love today. Amen

TRACY WILLIAMSON

A vital part of his body

If the whole body were an eye, where would the sense of hearing be? If the whole body were an ear, where would the sense of smell be? But in fact God has placed the parts in the body, every one of them, just as he wanted them to be. (NIV)

I remember once chatting with a Christian optician who said that the eye was so detailed and intricately made, that if he hadn't already been a Christian he would have become one just by seeing how truly awesome the eye and the wonder of sight are.

I found that incredible. There is so much we don't know about our bodies, but every tiny part, whether a cell, lens or valve, has as vital a role as the more obvious parts like the skin or organs. Those tiny parts are invisible, yet it is through their work that everything functions. Everything matters and is honoured. If any part is damaged, then everything else is affected.

When I was two, I had encephalitis which caused miniscule brain damage, leaving me with lifelong deafness, sight and balance problems. My ears are fine, but I cannot hear because of those damaged invisible brain cells. Everything matters in the body.

Paul wrote this allegory because of the competitiveness in the new church. This is a massive problem today too. We look up to those with recognised ministries and feel small in comparison. Our leaders may reinforce this lie, and sometimes we reinforce it too by always comparing ourselves negatively with others. I do this a lot. But God wants us to have a new vision of how much each person, including ourselves, matters. We are his body and every single part is there for a reason.

I believe God wants someone today to know that you are a vital part of his body. You are incredible. You may feel invisible, but God has woven things into your life that are both unique and essential for his body to truly function.

Think about baking a cake. What would happen if you left out one of the ingredients? What ingredients did God use to make you? What if he'd left one out? Thank him for making you, you.

TRACY WILLIAMSON

Gifted

There are different kinds of gifts, but the same Spirit distributes them. There are different kinds of service, but the same Lord. There are different kinds of working, but in all of them and in everyone it is the same God at work. (NIV)

In God's eyes you are gifted. You have a unique calling to reveal his love. You are anointed. I wonder if those words excite you or make you think, 'Me? I'm certainly not gifted!'

But this passage and many others show that you are important to God. We are all called to be Jesus' body in different ways, and he anoints us with special gifts through his Spirit to fulfil that calling.

My friend loves to bring gifts and chooses things that she knows Marilyn and I will like. She is so happy when we open our gifts and express our delight. God wants us to know that same delight in his gifts.

Paul says: 'To each one the manifestation of the Spirit is given for the common good.' Each one, that means you too!

'The manifestation' means the signs or the outworking of the Spirit's presence. God has gifted you with a unique outworking of the Spirit's presence. This could be through your ability with finance, your hospitable nature, your compassion or creativity, your ability to share prophetically, your musicianship, your teaching ability and so on. He has given you gifts that he knows will suit you.

As I was writing this, I sensed there is someone who was never given a gift when they were a child. What you hoped for never came and you felt deeply rejected. You cannot believe that God will give you anything. As I prayed, I saw a picture of a beautiful parcel with your name on. Inside there were many seeds which shone with glorious light and colour. They were symbolic of your calling. As you listen for God's counsel and plant those seeds in people's lives, I saw them growing into wonderful trees. You are gifted with care and empathy to give his love away in beautiful ways.

God delights to give you precious gifts. Imagine him giving you that beautiful parcel. Using these verses and also Romans 12:5–13, prayerfully 'open' your parcel to discover your gift. What does it look like? How will you use it?

TRACY WILLIAMSON

Mighty warrior

The angel of the Lord came and sat down under the oak in Ophrah that belonged to Joash the Abiezrite, where his son Gideon was threshing wheat in a winepress to keep it from the Midianites. When the angel of the Lord appeared to Gideon, he said, 'The Lord is with you, mighty warrior.' (NIV)

I love how the Lord declares things over us that humanly are not evident! Gideon was no mighty warrior, yet the Lord gave him that name because he had created Gideon to be courageous, mighty in doing his works and overcoming all opposition.

As I write, we are in the middle of the coronavirus pandemic, and, like Gideon, we are hiding – not in a winepress, but in our homes. It was unnatural for Gideon to thresh wheat in a winepress and this lockdown is unnatural too. I don't know what situations you are facing today, but God calls you Mighty Warrior. It is a name that belongs to us all because of the war we are in against Satan.

What do you most fear? With my deafness and experiences of rejection, I can really struggle with anxiety in social situations. When Marilyn first asked me to share my testimony, I was terrified. Here we see how God dealt patiently with Gideon's massive need for validation but refused to let him off the hook. In the same way, I knew God wanted me to push through my fear, trusting in his help to stand up and speak. As I did, amazingly, the Lord gave me a fluency and power to speak that I would never have thought possible. The fear lifted and instead I felt a longing to communicate God's amazing love. He had made me a mighty warrior, not against an army but against my personal restrictions.

The angel told Gideon, 'The Lord is with you.' This is the key to us living in his power rather than in fear. What lies does the devil whisper to you? The Lord is with you and has taken those lies to the cross. Your name is Mighty Warrior.

Are you fearful? Remember Jesus is with you and through his Spirit you are more than a conqueror. Listen to him. Are there things he is putting on your heart to do? What steps does he want you to take?

TRACY WILLIAMSON

Christ's ambassador

And he has committed to us the message of reconciliation. We are therefore Christ's ambassadors, as though God were making his appeal through us. We implore you on Christ's behalf: be reconciled to God. (NIV)

If you feel that you have no purpose as a Christian, this passage is an important one to reflect upon. An ambassador represents her country or a brand, caring deeply both for what they represent and for making them known.

Paul describes us as Christ's ambassadors who have been given 'the ministry of reconciliation'. God places huge trust in us. He says, 'I have chosen you to show people my love and to bring them home to me.' It's all about love: love for the one you represent and love for those around you. How that love will be expressed will vary hugely depending on your unique gifts and personality, but you will, in effect, be Jesus to them.

I came to know Christ through an amazing girl called Ruth. I was a student and was very depressed because of childhood abuse. One night I attempted suicide but failed. I didn't tell anyone, but a week later Ruth told me that she was a Christian, and that while she'd been praying God had put on her heart to tell me that he loved me. I was stunned. As Ruth shared more about the wonder of Jesus dying for me, her face was glowing. I could tell she loved and knew Jesus. Letting his love flow through her to me created a doorway and soon afterwards I became a Christian.

A Christian couple also had a transforming impact on me. I was still struggling with depression and one night ran away. After wandering many miles in torrential rain, I ended up on their doorstep at midnight. They responded with such compassion and care that I felt the Father's love and started my journey to healing. In different ways all three were used as ambassadors for Christ. How does he want to use you?

How did you find faith in God and how have other Christians helped you to go deeper? Thank God for them. Then, ask him how he wants you to be his ambassador. Pray he will give you lovely opportunities to step out.

TRACY WILLIAMSON

A living stone

You also, like living stones, are being built into a spiritual house to be a holy priesthood, offering spiritual sacrifices acceptable to God... You are a chosen people, a royal priesthood, a holy nation, God's special possession. (NIV)

The Lord once gave me an awesome vision through these verses. I have précised it here for you.

I saw a beautiful tower being built. It glowed with incandescent light that transformed the darkness. Its very stones were exuding radiance and each had a unique colour and shape. The Lord said, 'This is my dwelling place, the lives of those whom I love and died for. They are being formed into an invincible tower that is called by my name and will reveal my glory in the darkest places.'

Then I saw Jesus searching for the stones. With his bare hands he tore rubble apart to rescue each stone. One was badly misshapen. He said, 'This is someone who has been crushed.' Another was full of broken glass. He cradled it saying, 'This person has been very hurt.' He held them gently, loving them. Amazingly the rough edges became smooth and a beautiful colour shone through them. He placed them in the growing tower and each one fitted perfectly, enhancing the others' beauty and uniqueness, upholding those around it while also being upheld. It was a beautiful picture of mutual support with each stone playing a vital part.

As I continued to pray, I saw something that was deeply grieving him. Some stones were leaping out of the tower. One said, 'I'm too ugly.' Others said, 'We don't want to be there, we want to be here where we can glorify God.'

Jesus wept. 'Can't you see?' he said. 'The tower is beautiful because in your uniqueness you are a whole. On your own you are just one, but together you become a tower that even the satanic hosts cannot break down.'

But the stones wouldn't listen, saying, 'We don't like being with those stones, they're different to us.'

'In him the whole building is joined together and rises to become a holy temple in the Lord. And in him you too are being built together to become a dwelling in which God lives by his Spirit' (Ephesians 2:21–22, NIV). Are you?

TRACY WILLIAMSON

A new name

You'll get a brand-new name straight from the mouth of God. You'll be a stunning crown in the palm of God's hand, a jewelled gold cup held high in the hand of your God. No more will anyone call you Rejected… You''ll be called Hephzibah (My Delight). (MSG)

What is your name?

To the Jews every name was meaningful: Jesus meant Saviour, Abram meant Exalted Father and Abraham meant Father of Multitudes. Today, we often name our children according to fashion, but even so our names were always known by God, just as our genetic imprint was lovingly designed by him.

So naming is tied to our identity. Here, God is telling Jerusalem that her true name is 'Delighted-in Bride'. On a deeper level, that name belongs to us. Just as God told Jerusalem that her name was no longer 'Rejected', so he takes our old destructive 'names' and replaces them with our true identity because Jesus' death for us on the cross makes us 'new creations' (2 Corinthians 5:17).

When you look in the mirror, what names come to mind? I grew up hearing so often that I was mental, lazy, ugly, a failure… that these words became my identity. I even hated my actual name, Tracy, because my 'friend' said she thought it fitted that I had a meaningless name! I was shocked. Was I a meaningless person? I forgot her remark, but its message went into my heart along with all the others.

Thirty-five years later, God spoke a new name into my heart: Daughter of Mercy. I was overcome. God was saying that I belonged to him as a precious daughter and had a calling to give his mercy away to others. This is my true identity. Later, I found that Tracy does have a meaning – Domain, an area of influence. When I saw those first three letters of Domain, I saw D O M – Daughter of Mercy. How awesome! In him all things come together. I now know and seek to live out my true identity, Daughter of Mercy.

Give Jesus the wounding, negative 'names' you are holding on to and thank him for the beautiful name he gives you. Ask him to speak it over you. Write it down and ask Jesus to help you live in the truth of your new name.

TRACY WILLIAMSON

Powerful pray-er

Therefore, confess your sins to one another… and pray for one another, that you may be healed *and* restored. The heartfelt *and* persistent prayer of a righteous man (believer) can accomplish much… It is dynamic and can have tremendous power. (AMP)

Do you ever feel helpless when facing irrevocable situations? The economic and social cost of the coronavirus pandemic has been so profound that global recovery seems impossible.

But God has given us an amazing weapon: prayer. James explains that the power of prayer does not depend on our spirituality, but on our righteousness through Jesus, who empowers us to hear his voice and pray with authority.

Paul teaches us that even our tears will be turned by the Holy Spirit into prayer that touches God's heart and releases his divine power into the need. The key is to pray persistently with expectation.

I love how James emphasises Elijah's frailty. He too knew weakness, but as he listened to God and prayed accordingly, and amazing things happened.

When I first knew Marilyn, she had a very bad back and was in a wheelchair. People were praying but it just got worse. I felt grieved to see her in such pain, but my prayers felt futile, just words hitting the ceiling.

One night I dreamed that Marilyn and I were walking all the way down our local high street. We'd never been able to do this, but in the dream Marilyn was walking upright with no pain, laughing and enjoying shopping. When I awoke, I felt sad, thinking it was just a dream, but God said, 'Pray it into reality.' Over several months I kept praying that the dream would be made real. During that time, amazingly, God opened doors for Marilyn to have several weeks of treatment from a prayerful Christian chiropractor.

A year later Marilyn and I were walking down our local high street. She was laughing, walking upright and enjoying shopping. Suddenly I had an amazing sense of déjà vu. God had answered our prayers!

James said: 'Is anyone of you in trouble? You should pray.' Are you or someone you love in trouble? God will use your prayers and tears. Ask the Spirit, your Counsellor, to show you how to pray, and then pray!

TRACY WILLIAMSON

Tree of life

His pleasure and passion is remaining true to the Word of 'I Am,' meditating day and night in the true revelation of light. He will stand firm like a flourishing tree planted by God's design, deeply rooted by the brooks of bliss, bearing fruit in every season of his life. (TPT)

How wonderful that God describes us as a tree! Here the image is of a tree planted by the brook; in Isaiah 61:3, we are 'oaks of righteousness... for the display of his splendour' (NIV) and in John 15, a branch of the vine. They are pictures of our calling to reveal God and make his love known, to bear lasting fruit, to drink in and cling to God's goodness.

Trees are majestic and life-giving. Tall and strong, they give shelter and their beauty calms the soul. Their leaves and blossom are gloriously rich with colour. Some trees feed us with nourishing fruit; others give their wood. As high as a tree grows, so its roots must go deep into the ground, gripping the earth and drinking in its nutrients. By its very stance, a tree communicates worship.

What does our life stance communicate? I remember once feeling furious with a bus that was late. By the time I got home I was in a bad mood. I tried to empty the bin but couldn't open the bin bag, so I shook it violently, scaring the cat. The thought came: 'What a grumpy old bag you are. Where's your thankfulness?' I was shocked as I realised I had reacted in a very self-pitying way, forgetting the Lord was with me. I asked him to forgive me and to help me see life through his eyes of thankfulness. I was amazed as I began to notice beautiful happenings all around me, such as a streetwise teenager stopping to help an old lady.

Similarly, this psalmist calls us to make good choices. In our daily lives, do we drink in Jesus' true life-giving words or Satan's lies? Are our hearts filled with God's love or the world's default of judgement and criticism? Are we grumpy or thankful?

Lord, thank you that you see me as a tree, revealing your splendour, drinking in your love, putting my roots deeper into your truth, bearing life-giving fruit. Please work in me to make my life full of your thankfulness and love. Amen
TRACY WILLIAMSON

Known, loved and wonderfully made

You formed my innermost being, shaping my delicate inside and my intricate outside, and wove them all together in my mother's womb. I thank you, God, for making me so mysteriously complex! Everything you do is marvellously breathtaking. (TPT)

David begins by reflecting on how deeply God knows him: 'You read my heart like an open book and you know all the words I'm about to speak before I even start a sentence.'

Do you find that scary? For David it brings an awesome awareness of God's love for him. I love my dog Goldie and know all his little ways. Those of you with children sometimes just gaze at them, loving who they are.

God loves you and therefore knows all your ways. He is with you when you celebrate; he is close by when you weep. He loves who you are. And so, we come full circle. We began our study thinking about how God had always planned for us to belong to him; now we see his delight in creating us, weaving together all the intricate details that make us unique.

Never let the enemy convince you that you are inferior. We all need Jesus. We make wrong choices and life sometimes robs us, but when God made us he saw that we were 'very good' (Genesis 1:31). He made your gender, your hair colour, your way of thinking, your athletic ability.

Do you enjoy creating? God made us in his image, so creativity is a central part of our make-up. Marilyn loves to create beautiful songs. I love threading words together to express amazing truths. I have artist friends who paint incredible pictures, photographer friends who take breathtaking photos, friends who turn business into an adventure and friends who inject joy into every activity.

What thrills your heart? No two artists are the same unless they deliberately copy each other's work. God hasn't created you as a copy but, as Paul describes, 'God's masterpiece' (Ephesians 2:10, NLT). This is you. Can you accept and celebrate it?

Read this psalm afresh reflecting on all that God has been saying to you over this fortnight. Thank him for every truth which reveals who we are. Ask him to help you live in those truths.

TRACY WILLIAMSON

Daily essentials for believers

Christine Platt writes:

This title can sound a bit daunting, but I think we could summarise the essentials of living a meaningful life with God as: love God and love people. This is a constructive summary of what we should aim for each day of our lives as followers of Jesus. God wants us to succeed in our faith journey and has given us many pointers and clues to help us on our way. We will be looking at 14 of these in our study.

This is not meant to be a list of dos and don'ts. These reflections represent some of God's wisdom about how to navigate our way as Christians in this world which, much of the time, seeks to hinder rather than help us.

God has not left us to struggle alone. We have the Bible, other believers and supremely the Holy Spirit, whose fundamental desire and mission in life is to help us. We could ask ourselves: with all those resources available, how could we fail? But we all do from time to time. To walk with God is not easy but it is the most fulfilling lifestyle we could have. So it's sensible to take advantage of all the help on offer, just as we would with any other learning opportunity. It would be downright foolish and dangerous to jump into a car and speed off without learning to drive. We'd be a menace to ourselves and others. Similarly, we have much to learn about how to walk with God, so we should not ignore his coaching. To do so will bring pain and frustration to ourselves, those who love us and our Father himself.

Thankfully, God is patient with fallible humanity. He announced himself to Moses as 'the God of compassion and mercy! I am slow to anger and filled with unfailing love and faithfulness' (Exodus 34:6, NLT). I find it helpful to visualise the Christian life as a journey with ups and downs, twists and turns, but always steering onward and upward towards God and our ultimate destination to be with him forever.

So let me encourage us all to take these thoughts to heart and to not get discouraged at setbacks. Let us place ourselves in the arms of God, who is patient and compassionate, and filled with unfailing love and faithfulness.

Trust God

Search for the Lord and for his strength; continually seek him. (NLT)

The first essential is to trust God. Any discussion about trust relies on the trustworthiness of the person or object. We put our trust in all manner of things: planes, chairs, as well as surgeons, dentists, etc. With a recent broken arm, I had to submit myself to the expertise of a surgeon. I couldn't offer my advice or opinion during the operation as I was blissfully anaesthetised! You trust the hospital has confidence in their staff's abilities and qualifications. All went well!

Is God trustworthy? The psalmist encourages us to reflect on who God is and what he has done ('Remember the wonders he has performed, his miracles, and the rulings he has given', v. 5) and also to remember that 'he is the Lord our God' (v. 7). Reminding ourselves of God's character of love, power and faithfulness, and of his answers to prayer will give us a strong foundation on which to build even deeper trust.

This must be an ongoing process: 'Continually seek him.' Every day we have new challenges to confront and need his presence and strength to face them. We will never get to the stage when we can manage on our own. God didn't design us that way. He has all the resources we will ever need for whatever happens, and he has proven his reliability a zillion times. Just think of Mary, the mother of Jesus, and how God enabled her to live her life of patient faith in those extraordinary circumstances.

One snag is that I so easily forget his goodness, so I try to regularly write in my journal to help me remember all he has done for me day by day – very encouraging to look back on.

Lord God, thank you for your faithfulness to me in the past. I seek your strength to continue to trust you and surrender myself to you for this day and all my days.

CHRISTINE PLATT

Study God's word

'**Study this Book of Instruction continually. Meditate on it day and night so you will be sure to obey everything written in it. Only then will you prosper and succeed in all you do.**' (NLT)

God gave Joshua a massive assignment. Moses was a spiritual giant and an incredibly hard act to follow. How did God encourage his new recruit? First, he promised to always be present with Joshua and, second, gave him this command – study, meditate upon and obey his word. That would be the key to Joshua's success, not military strategy or striving in his own strength.

Joshua was a busy man. He had a whole tribe of (sometimes rebellious) Israelites to guide, rivers to cross and cities to conquer. However, it seems he certainly made time to study and meditate on what God said.

The fact that you're reading this book indicates that you value God's word and consider it a daily necessity. I know it's tempting to just read the verse at the top and skim through the reflection, but let me urge you to read the whole passage and study it for yourself first. What is God saying to you today? Joshua didn't have daily notes to rely on. He had to study for himself, and he certainly prospered and succeeded in all he did. Few of us could claim to be busier than Joshua.

I've found memorising verses to be an indispensable stimulus to help keep God's word in my mind throughout the day. You could try having a verse as your screensaver or write one out on a card and stick it by the bathroom mirror. Let's try creative ways of studying and meditating on God's word continually. We are often surrounded by toxic negativity. Let's counteract those influences with the purity and positivity of what God says. The result will be success in our relationship with God.

What can you do today to study and meditate on God's word continually? Why not try one of the suggestions in this reflection.

CHRISTINE PLATT

Keep his commands

Don't just listen to God's word. You must do what it says. Otherwise, you are only fooling yourselves… If you do what it says and don't forget what you heard, then God will bless you for doing it. (NLT)

We would probably all agree that God knows best how we should live and what lifestyle will be the most exciting and fulfilling for us. Right from the beginning, in Exodus 20, he set out his commands which would guarantee rich, harmonious relationships with God and with each other. Doesn't that sound glorious?

All through the Bible we are urged to obey God's word – not just to know what he asks of us but to act on that knowledge. This principle applies in all areas of life. There is no point being able to recite the Highway Code and know the speed limits off by heart if we don't obey them. We could end up killing some poor innocent person and/or ourselves. The ghastly consequences of that disobedience are all around us.

As an incentive, there are delightful rewards promised if we obey. God will bless us (v. 25). In yesterday's reading God said he would give success to Joshua in all he did. Most importantly, we will have a closer understanding and experience of God. Jesus said: 'Those who accept my commandments and obey them are the ones who love me. And because they love me, my Father will love them. And I will love them and reveal myself to each of them' (John 14:21).

However, Jesus warns us that there will also be a cost. 'If any of you wants to be my follower, you must give up your own way, take up your cross, and follow me' (Matthew 16:24). We need to put aside our own plans and wants and be prepared to face the consequences. Other people may reject us and even hate us. Obedience is the way to go, however much of a struggle it is. We do not know best, but God does.

Is there an area of life where you know what God is saying but you're hesitating or resisting? God loves you so much and wants the best for you. Do you want to please God or Satan?

CHRISTINE PLATT

Persist in prayer

Pray in the Spirit at all times and on every occasion. Stay alert and be persistent in your prayers for all believers everywhere. (NLT)

Isn't it phenomenal that our omnipotent God gives us free access to chat with him? On a trip to the UK, I had the wonderful treat of visiting Buckingham Palace. There were several layers of security to go through. We also had to pay and book well ahead of time. Needless to say, the Queen wasn't in residence. We just saw part of her home and it was magnificent.

We pay nothing to talk with God, nor do we need an appointment. The only security check is 'Do you have faith?' Only a tiny bit will suffice. It's an awe-inspiring privilege, but also a command.

We are to pray in the Spirit – asking the Holy Spirit to guide our prayers – at all times and on every occasion. There is no moment when prayer is inappropriate or unnecessary. Even when we're busy with other activities, part of our minds can tune in to God and ask for his help, guidance and strength for the task or opportunity in hand. I have often sent an arrow prayer to God in the middle of a conversation with someone when I've no idea what to say.

The Lord's Prayer is a helpful model to follow (Matthew 6:9–13). It starts with praise. That lifts our thoughts above the problem. We ask for forgiveness and for daily needs, provision and protection, for ourselves and others. If you write down what you pray for, it's encouraging to look back and see how God has answered. It also helps us to remember to say thank you.

Maybe some of us feel our prayer lives are inadequate. Satan would love us to get discouraged and give up. Verse 13 of the Lord's Prayer says, 'Rescue us from the evil one.'

Try using this quote to help you see the huge potential of your prayers: 'To clasp the hands in prayer is the beginning of an uprising against the disorder of the world' (Karl Barth, 1886–1968).

CHRISTINE PLATT

Use your armour

Put on all of God's armour so that you will be able to stand firm against all strategies of the devil. For we are not fighting against flesh-and-blood enemies, but against evil rulers and authorities of the unseen world, against mighty powers in this dark world. (NLT)

Any military commander would give their eye teeth to know the enemy's tactics and plan of attack. The cracking of the Nazi Enigma code was a major turning point in World War II, giving the Allies advance warning of Nazi plans.

Jesus leaves us in no doubt as to who our enemy is and his strategies. He is described as a lion seeking to devour (1 Peter 5:8). In the natural world the lion is the king of the jungle. In the spiritual world Jesus is king and Satan is a defeated foe. But we know that Satan doesn't play nicely and will keep on attacking God's people until the very end. He hates God with a passion and his plan is to discourage and destroy what God loves – us! God has not left us helpless in the face of this formidable antagonist. It is essential that we use all the armour he provides.

I recently became aware that I tend to imagine catastrophic situations. I think of all that might go wrong and work out how I'll cope with that. Eventually I realised this was an enemy attack to distract and harass me and cause me to focus on negative possibilities. Now I aim to put on the belt of truth and use the shield of faith to refute those imaginary scenarios. However, I know that Satan and his minions have many more vile schemes to find cracks in my armour. So, I must be armed and alert.

Even in the Lord's Prayer Jesus reminds us about this essential area of being a disciple; 'And don't let us yield to temptation but rescue us from the evil one' (Matthew 6:13).

I praise you, Jesus, that you have defeated Satan. Help me to become more aware of the way he attacks me and to take up all the armour you've provided.

CHRISTINE PLATT

Do good

Always try to do good to each other and to all people… Hold on to what is good. Stay away from every kind of evil. (NLT)

The apostle Peter summed up Jesus' lifestyle like this: 'Jesus went around doing good' (Acts 10:38). From what we know of how he spent his days, 'doing good' included listening to people with compassion, teaching God's ways, healing the sick and demonised, confronting people with their sinful behaviour, encouraging people to grow in faith and, supremely, loving sacrificially.

In the context of our reading in 1 Thessalonians, doing good involves respecting our leaders, living peacefully with others, warning the lazy, encouraging the timid, caring tenderly for the weak and being patient with everyone. I would love this to be my epitaph: 'She went around doing good.' How cool would it be to know that I contributed to making the world a kinder place by doing good for someone.

It takes wisdom to discern exactly what is good for individuals. You might notice people in church who are pew-sitters and not volunteering for any service. One might be lazy; another might lack self-confidence and fear doing it wrong or not being considered worthy; still another might be so overwhelmed with troubles that they can't see beyond their own burdens. One size does not fit all.

I remember to my shame trying to encourage a friend to strive for a better job by doing a computer course to make herself more employable. Eventually she confided that she didn't have the intellectual capacity to do it. I felt so bad that I hadn't asked more questions to begin with, rather than assume I knew what was best for her. So, instead of doing good, I did the opposite. I embarrassed her and emphasised her limitations. Not good at all.

Lord, teach me how to do good to all whom I meet today. Open my eyes to their needs and lead me by your Holy Spirit to serve in the most loving and constructive way.

CHRISTINE PLATT

Serve with enthusiasm

Thank God! He gives us victory over sin and death through our Lord Jesus Christ. So… be strong and immovable. Always work enthusiastically for the Lord, for you know that nothing you do for the Lord is ever useless. (NLT)

When I finally gave my life to Jesus, one of the truths that drew me was that knowing God gives life ultimate meaning. Without God or eternal hope for life beyond our earthly existence, it all seemed a bit pointless. We are born, we pack as much life as possible into our allotted time and then we die. Some people achieve fame and fortune or make a life-changing medical discovery. Most of us are pretty ordinary. Is that enough?

In this passage Paul teaches about a whole new dimension of life after this one, when believers will be given imperishable, spiritual, powerful and glorious bodies which will last forever, and we will live with God himself. That's the motivation of verse 58. Because of the resurrection we are to be strong and immovable, and always work enthusiastically for the Lord. Nothing we do for him is useless, even if we don't see immediate results. God doesn't call us to be successful. He does call us to be faithful and to leave the outcome to him.

I have recently looked back over my life of walking with Jesus. I remembered my weekly visits to a prison in West Africa. It was an exceedingly dark place, both physically and spiritually, but there were glimmers of faith and hope. I didn't know at the time whether anything was achieved for God's kingdom, but with the eye of faith I fully expect some joyous reunions with redeemed ex-convicts when I get to heaven. I didn't always want to go and face the sadness or the smell, but I did sense God not only going with me but being already present in that prison. The reality of heaven makes my small contribution worth it.

Memorise this verse if you are tempted to lose heart in your service for Jesus: 'Always work enthusiastically for the Lord, for you know that nothing you do for the Lord is ever useless.'

CHRISTINE PLATT

Be ready to explain your faith

Through thick and thin, keep your hearts at attention, in adoration before Christ, your Master. Be ready to speak up and tell anyone who asks why you're living the way you are, and always with the utmost courtesy. (MSG)

As I was studying this passage, I noticed for the first time that this well-known verse about being ready to explain the gospel to others is topped and tailed by verses about suffering. We only have to think of the persecuted church of today, as well as biblical heroes and heroines like Stephen, Paul, Priscilla and Aquila, to realise that speaking out about Christ can lead to suffering.

One of my icons of courageous witness is Corrie ten Boon, a Dutch believer who, with her family, enabled Jews to escape the Nazi Holocaust. She was imprisoned in Ravensbrück concentration camp – unimaginable horror. Jesus is, of course, the supreme example of suffering. 'He went through it all – was put to death and then made alive – to bring us to God.' In readying ourselves to share our hope, we need also to be prepared to suffer. Maybe our suffering will include the loss of friendships, ridicule, sarcasm or much worse.

In order to be able to speak up we need to be clear about what to say. Preparing a short testimony will help get our thoughts in order. Let's be faithful in doing our homework.

The key to being asked about our beliefs is that our lifestyle should invite comment. How often do people ask you: 'Why do you live like that?' I confess for me it is seldom. That can feel discouraging, but I think people do notice even if they don't want to talk about it. There may come a time when they will ask and be open to listen. It's our daily lives as well as our words that are important, although we don't want to stand out as being odd or weird. I often pray that something of Jesus might be evident in my conversation, values and attitudes.

Lord Jesus, thank you for the wonderful message of hope and love that I can share with my family, friends and neighbours. Please give me opportunities and the wisdom and winsomeness to communicate something of you.

CHRISTINE PLATT

Be full of joy in the Lord

Always be full of joy in the Lord. I say it again – rejoice!... Remember, the Lord is coming soon. Don't worry about anything; instead pray about everything. (NLT)

Joy is another significant guideline for a satisfying life with Christ. However, there are many ghastly things that cause us grief and anger in our personal worlds and in the wider world. So, how can we possibly always be joyful? Jesus, through Paul, gives us some sources of gladness.

First, the Lord is coming soon. Other translations phrase it as 'The Lord is near'. Either way, it is hugely encouraging. Any day now Jesus could split the heavens and return in a blaze of majestic glory. While we wait for that cataclysmic event, Jesus reassures us that he is near. He is approachable. He is listening. He is ready to support and guide us. We are within easy reach of his mercy and love.

Second, we can pray about whatever is disturbing us, be it starving children or annoying family members. At times I pray but feel no relief. Joyce Meyer points out: 'The word does not instruct us to pray with complaining; it says to pray with thanksgiving' (*The Everyday Life Bible*, Amplified Bible with notes by Joyce Meyer). Ouch. How many times have I brought my moans to God and not my thanks?

Third, a joyful attitude is rooted in what we think about. We need to fill our minds with truth – 'the best, not the worst; the beautiful, not the ugly' (v. 8, MSG). This morning I spent some minutes reading a story on my Google newsfeed. Not only did I waste time, but I was bombarded with adverts and probably fake news. Our brains are precious gifts from God and should be treated with care and protected from attack, filled with good news. This brings peace and for that we can be very glad.

Lord, there is so much to be glad about, but I sometimes feel angry and upset. Help me to focus my mind on you and your truth so that joy, the fruit of your Holy Spirit, might grow in me.

CHRISTINE PLATT

Always be gentle

I... beg you to lead a life worthy of your calling, for you have been called by God. Always be humble and gentle. Be patient with each other, making allowance for each other's faults because of your love. (NLT)

When I think about gentleness I am reminded of when God spoke to an exceedingly discouraged and depressed Elijah. He had fled to the wilderness after Jezebel had threatened to kill him (1 Kings 19:3–18). Emotionally and physically exhausted, he went 'alone into the wilderness... and prayed that he might die'. God sent an angel on takeaway duty to provide sustaining food and drink. God then met with Elijah on Mount Sinai. First, there was a howling windstorm, then an earthquake and then fire. Elijah didn't respond to any of those, but when he heard a gentle whisper, he recognised the voice of God.

Gentleness is not weakness. It is a fruit of the Holy Spirit (Galatians 5:23). Other similar qualities include meekness, unselfishness, humility and tenderness. Elijah didn't need a demonstration of God's overwhelming power; he needed a comforting arm around his shoulder encouraging and strengthening him to persevere as God's prophet.

I think we could all do with more gentleness to cope with this harsh world in which we live. Do you sometimes find you are tempted to judge people and want to give them a good kick to sort themselves out if they seem to be making unwise decisions? I know I do. I need to remind myself that I don't know their backstory. Maybe a hug would be more beneficial than a kick.

For some of us, the person in our lives towards whom we should show more gentleness is ourselves. Are there voices in your head accusing you of not measuring up, commanding you to do more, pray more, love more? That's exhausting. We are to 'be patient with each other [including ourselves], making allowance for each other's faults'.

How can you make the world a gentler place for yourself and those around you today? Try memorising this verse: 'Always be humble and gentle.'

CHRISTINE PLATT

Use your words well

Live wisely among those who are not believers, and make the most of every opportunity. Let your conversation be gracious and attractive so that you will have the right response for everyone. (NLT)

As a new believer I remember having verbal tussles with people. I felt it was my responsibility to argue them into the kingdom. Needless to say, this did not work well for me or for them. I was frustrated at their stubbornness to understand and believe. They were no doubt offended by my lack of basic politeness and unwillingness to listen to their point of view. I wasn't answering the questions they were asking. I was giving them the information I thought they needed. Bad idea.

Verses like today's reading can sometimes have a paralysing effect. How can I have the right response for everyone? Is it better to stay silent if I'm stuck for the right response? One of the most helpful guidelines for evangelism I was taught is: It's okay to say, 'I don't know, but I will try to find that answer for you.' It would be wonderful to be an expert on all things spiritual, but it's unrealistic. Even when I read well-researched books on creation, suffering or the end times, I can't always recall the salient facts at the right time. Often, it's better to lend people the helpful book rather than try to paraphrase someone's thorough in-depth study on a subject in a few rather inadequate sentences of my own.

This verse is written in the context of sharing the gospel, but it's also a good guideline for everyday conversation. Some of what we hear in the media and from those around us can be coarse and unkind. I find I need to be alert, to not let it affect how I talk to others and about others. It's not cool to be sarcastic or disrespectful.

Lord, may my conversation today be gracious and attractive. Help me to remember that you are listening. You are the unseen participant in all my interactions.

CHRISTINE PLATT

Always give thanks

Enter his gates with thanksgiving; go into his courts with praise. Give thanks to him and praise his name. For the Lord is good. His unfailing love continues forever, and his faithfulness continues to each generation. (NLT)

If you search the internet for 'give thanks to God', you are spoilt for choice. It's clear that being thankful is very important to him. Why is that? Why is he so keen for us to say thank you?

On a mundane level, we all like to be thanked for the things we do. Otherwise, we feel unappreciated. I don't think God is emotionally dependent upon us saying thank you. He wants us to be thankful because he knows it is good for us.

I have recently been in contact with someone who is deeply depressed. Everything she said and did was negative. No matter what we suggested, she couldn't see anything good in the past, present or future. It was unbearably sad. She was so unhappy. Obviously, she is an extreme case and needs spiritual, medical and psychological intervention.

Without wanting to downplay clinical depression, the principle is that if we deliberately decide to be thankful to God and to others, especially when we don't feel like it, that will boost our emotional well-being. This alters our outlook on life and brings a greater sense of joy and peace. We are to 'enter his gates with thanksgiving', or as *The Message* puts it, 'Enter with the password, "Thank you!"' What are his gates? The context implies the temple gates. Now I think it refers to approaching his presence. We start off our days and our prayers with thanks. Even if you only have a moment, the best prayer is: 'Thank you, God.'

Verses 3 and 5 give us several reasons to be thankful. He is our good God. We are his well-tended sheep. He looks after us and promises to lead, protect and provide forever.

Use this psalm to remind you to be thankful to God, so that it becomes a natural habit to turn to God often during the day with a thankful heart.

CHRISTINE PLATT

Always be confident

So we are always confident, even though we know that as long as we live in these bodies we are not at home with the Lord. For we live by believing and not by seeing. Yes, we are fully confident. (NLT)

I vividly remember the first time I was asked to host a meeting. I was paralysed with fear. I wept with God, saying, 'I can't do that. What if I make a mess of it?' To my huge relief the planning team and I came to a compromise. I would do part of it and someone else would do the rest. So, with knocking knees and sweaty hands, I stepped forward and managed my bit. Over the intervening months I was given other opportunities to lead and, in the end, I began to enjoy it. A miracle! God helped me grow in confidence in that context as I faced the fear and did it anyway.

This passage talks about the confidence with which we can approach all of life's ups and downs because of Jesus and the unbelievably magnificent future he has prepared for his people. Like me, you may be finding that your physical body is causing you to 'groan and sigh', but all of God's people will receive glorious new bodies which will never die. The guarantee of this is God's gift of the majestic, ever-present Holy Spirit.

This is how we can always be confident: the Holy Spirit is constantly with us, guiding, protecting and holding us up. Even if things fall apart, he does not give up on us but reassures us that we have a thoroughly successful future to look forward to in heaven. We may not always feel confident, but 'we live by believing and not by seeing'.

I am grateful that I was pushed out of my comfort zone to learn to lean on God and be confident in many other potentially terrifying moments.

What occasions give you the collywobbles? Is there some way you could start small and grow in confidence, relying on the Holy Spirit's help and support? Remember God's guarantee of your future in eternity.

CHRISTINE PLATT

Hold tightly to hope

Our guilty consciences have been sprinkled with Christ's blood to make us clean… Let us hold tightly without wavering to the hope we affirm, for God can be trusted to keep his promise. (NLT)

As I write, Susan, the adult daughter of a friend of mine, is currently in a hospice with liver failure. The transplant didn't work. She has just a few days to live. Her deep faith in God has sustained her over a lifetime of ill health. A grieving neighbour said, 'It's so sad. She's too young to die.' This is where the rubber hits the road. I attempted to explain that, although we grieve, Susan has an unbelievably wonderful future in heaven with no pain or illness. We feel desperately sad for those who are left, but not for Susan. She will pass into the presence of God and into a place of joy, peace and beauty, able to renew friendships with those who have gone before. Perfect paradise.

Because of Jesus we can be certain of this hope of heaven and therefore we hold tightly without wavering to the hope we affirm, for God can be trusted to keep his promise.

My grieving neighbour couldn't accept this. She was focused only on this life and had no hope for eternity. No wonder she was distraught. It's a challenge to believe in something we cannot see, but we have God's promise. Jesus is preparing a place for all his people (John 14:1–3). He died to make it possible for us to be forgiven and cleansed from all sin so that we can boldly enter into heaven's Most Holy Place. My neighbour tried to argue me out of this hope. Many people will attempt that, which is why scripture urges us to 'hold tightly without wavering'.

Over the past two weeks we have looked at 14 essentials. If we persevere in putting these into practice, they will build our faith and enable us to 'hold tightly' when opposition comes.

Thank you, mighty Jesus, for your immense sacrifice for me so that I can look forward with sure and certain hope for a gloriously happy eternity with you.

CHRISTINE PLATT

God's gift of peace

Victoria Byrne writes:

I invite you to reflect on peace.

Most of these thoughts were written in the spring of 2020 during the Covid-19 lockdown, when people throughout the world were told to stay in their homes. Though I can't know what life will be like by the time you read this, I know that life never stays still. We all go through seasons when peace feels harder to access. This season has been quieter for me, but it has forced me to confront my relationship with God and ask myself how much I am taking up his offer of peace.

When challenges come, do you engage well with God? Do you easily access his peace? Do you find you distract yourself with activity instead, or retreat into numbness or worry? What would be your definition of peace? One aspect I have not focused on is world peace. Instead we will 'start at home' and focus on our inner peace and the health of our relationships with other people and God. Not all the passages we will cover mention peace explicitly, but they lead us into the many ways that God brings us into well-being – shalom.

My feeling is that finding contentment is easier if our goal in life is to have the kind of peace that God wants – a trusting, life-filled flourishing of mind and body, rather than an expectation that God will free us of all challenges. After all, any activity has its stresses and challenges. Even children enjoying a kickabout in a sunny park are exerting themselves and making small decisions at every moment. Likewise, we're not looking for a peace that is like one endless perfect moment in an imaginary picture of holiness; we are trying to live like Jesus, who was real and dealt with difficulties, but was at peace with his heavenly Father and kept his peace even in storms and among accusers.

Perhaps as we enter into this subject, the best thing we can do is to pray for ourselves and each other. May we grow in strength to identify and take captive the unhelpful thoughts that rob us of God's gift. May we draw closer to Christ, who is our peace. May we delight in how he has enabled us to be at peace with him. May we learn to be gentle with ourselves as we go.

First things first

He reached down from on high and took hold of me; he drew me out of deep waters. He rescued me from my powerful enemy, from my foes, who were too strong for me. (NIV)

Lately, I'm finding peace quite hard to come by. A seemingly small leasehold decision made years ago now threatens to be pressing and expensive. Other unknowns are distracting me from God's promises, making me constantly feel like I should be taking action. Normally I just focus on my daily duties, doing what I can and leaving the rest to God. But I'll admit, my priority this week has been financial security. I've worried that our security has vanished because real life is more expensive than I thought.

God has powerfully reminded me that he is my top priority. So issues with our home pale into insignificance; it is much more important that we are doing what God wants us to be doing. How I'm treating my family matters more, and that's good because there's much love in this home.

This passage gives us a renewed sense of God's power and perspective. His awareness of us is like someone watching over us from high above. We are not hidden from him in a deep valley, even if we wanted to be ('Where can I flee from your presence?', Psalm 139:7). God's great love and his great power mean that we are safe. Though we are weak, he is strong. Although we may worry that we have no voice, in fact we have the ear of the Lord of Lords and we can hear his voice too. Although we get lost, he always knows the right way, so let's trust him. We may easily wander off the path, like sheep, but our shepherd is happy to leave the wise sheep in order to find the one that has become entangled in trouble.

Lord, you know my foolish ways, but you are always kind and you help me. Remind me hourly to reach for your hand to guide me through the churning waters of this season.

VICTORIA BYRNE

Being about our Father's business

Now the donkeys belonging to Saul's father Kish were lost, and Kish said to his son Saul, 'Take one of the servants with you and go and look for the donkeys'... [Samuel] kissed him, saying, 'Has not the Lord anointed you ruler over his inheritance?' (NIV)

I have been mulling over the process of God's guidance. I'm struck by the peace that comes from doing God's will, in matters large and small. The trick is to find God's will, so how do we do that?

Today's passage begins with Saul obeying his father's orders and ends with his discovering that he is doing God's will. In a sense, he doesn't know the difference. He is about his father's business looking for the donkeys. With the help of his godly servant, who suggests they ask the prophet for guidance, he walks into a situation that God has arranged.

There's a wonderful reminder that God sets us up for success as we go about our daily duties. Saul could be seen as a passive figure in this account, but this isn't a bad thing in this context. As the story plays out, it is clear that God was a step ahead of them all the way. Despite Saul's fears, he participates in what God has ordained.

In the passage, we're reminded of how intertwined the father's needs are with the son's duties. Kish's animals are lost, so it's Saul's job to find them. Through this account God shows us how he can be working behind the scenes. As Saul carries out the necessary tasks in front of him, God is executing his plan for them to participate in a greater journey. We can take fresh encouragement to welcome our duties because they are often the way God helps and guides us. In the same way, Saul's dedication to being about his father's immediate business leads him unknowingly into taking part in the plan God had designed for Saul's life, which would affect the nation.

'Trust in the Lord with all your heart and lean not on your own understanding; in all your ways submit to him, and he will make your paths straight' (Proverbs 3:5–6).

VICTORIA BYRNE

Strengthen ourselves in the Lord

But David found strength in the Lord his God. Then David said to Abiathar the priest, the son of Ahimelek, 'Bring me the ephod.' Abiathar brought it to him, and David enquired of the Lord, 'Shall I pursue this raiding party? Will I overtake them?' 'Pursue them,' he answered. (NIV)

In asking for the ephod, a garment priests would wear, David is signalling his intent to stop, listen and make his decision subject to the will of God. Immediately before this, David's mind was not at peace. David has just lost family members and others in battle, and he must now decide how his nation will respond to the enemy's attack. It's a decision that involves the safety of his people, and he does not know the right way forward. So, before choosing a course of action, he has stopped to 'find strength in the Lord his God'. In doing so, he reminds himself of who God is, and of their relationship.

I'm encouraged that this was an act of will for David, just as it is for any of us. We might imagine that the heroes and heroines of the Bible had an automatic, permanent confidence in God. This passage reminds me that it is always an act of will to connect with God.

As I sit here, contemplating the decisions that are required to navigate my own life, I concede I need to stop relying on my own abilities and instead, like David, ask God. Then my mind slowly becomes peaceful and I am able to hear what God is trying to tell me. There is a lot of interference and white noise for God's voice to overcome. On this occasion I stop and ask him about a series of decisions I need to make, and he jogs my memory about a happy video I watched earlier about planting peas. I feel like he's telling me to just take things step by step, and he will take it from there. That brings peace.

Does Jude's advice to build yourself up 'in your most holy faith', to pray in the Holy Spirit and to keep yourselves in God's love (Jude 1:20–21) help you find strength in your current circumstances?

VICTORIA BYRNE

Keeping our focus

This is what the Sovereign Lord, the Holy One of Israel, says: 'In repentance and rest is your salvation, in quietness and trust is your strength, but you would have none of it.' (NIV)

I find there are two equal and opposite states of mind which both draw me away from God's peace. In one I feel too busy; the other is like a warm bath of distraction and entertainment that lulls me into feeling like I don't need to connect with God at all.

I'm pondering the peaceful feelings I was having today because, although I have felt good, I have been avoiding God. So can it be a good kind of peace if I feel like I have been hiding from God? My study of shalom, the Hebrew word we translate as 'peace', shows that it is more like a deep flourishing, a mind-body-spirit holistic wellness out of which comes a display of his vibrant, abundant life.

I want to be peaceful, not anaesthetised! I'm grateful for this peaceful, sunny weekend, but I want to live in an engaged-with-God peace. I see now I've been thinking that engaging with God today would interrupt my peace. I need to offer up to him every season of life, to consider each one of them a season with its own purpose, instead of wanting life to be always exciting. God creates times of peace: the winter when seeds lie dormant; the warming earth in early spring, before the green shoots poke up; late summer when the seed heads mature in the warm sun, ready to let go and restart the cycle.

I'm going to give thanks for the way my life is right now, however it is. When life is busy, I will surely look back on the particular nature of this time I had and see in hindsight its blessings. Then I will be glad I enjoyed this day just as it was.

'This is the day that the Lord has made; let us rejoice and be glad in it' (Psalm 118:24, ESV).

VICTORIA BYRNE

The way to freedom and peace

Confess your sins to each other and pray for each other so that you may be healed. (NIV)

I was talking with church friends about how God's Holy Spirit works with us. We discovered we all had a struggle in common: we had all been avoiding certain emotional areas of life and effectively shutting God out of them. The conversation turned out to be deeply emotional, but we each felt safe and the result was liberating.

God's Holy Spirit had led each of us through very emotional times in recent months. We shared the stories of what had happened and the effect it had on us. As we talked it through, we saw what good things God had been doing, despite us trying to avoid the challenge. We saw that he was helping us become healthier, more emotional people.

We finished the conversation by praying together, and it was so good to be able to repent of having shut the door to various people or situations in our lives that had seemed too emotional to deal with. It felt particularly powerful to acknowledge those things to each other in that safe, mutual way and to hand that sin over to God together.

Confession may have brought momentary discomfort, but through it we experienced great peace and joy, all the greater because we discovered it together. That gave us proof of each other's continued loving regard, which reflects God's even greater love for us. Forgiveness brings peace and can even bring physical healing, according to friends who have witnessed that. Perhaps we underestimate how much is going on in our passage today, which is often quoted as a way to get healed, but rarely as an exploration of a community learning to live at peace internally and externally.

Do you have a friend you can be deeply honest with, with whom you can pray? If not, ask God to bring such a friendship into your life.

VICTORIA BYRNE

God's mission

'To shine on those living in darkness and in the shadow of death, to guide our feet into the path of peace.' (NIV)

Today we look at the big picture of God's desire for peace with us. When Jesus physically arrived on earth, God began a new display of his attitude of peace towards *anthropos*: humans. Angels sang to the startled shepherds on the hillside with these immortal words: 'Glory to God in the highest heaven, and on earth peace to those on whom his favour rests' (Luke 2:14). God offers his peace to those who wish to accept it, to people of good will. Anyone can choose to be included. God longs to be close to all those he made.

How can I better collaborate with him on that? God is always trying to re-establish that peace with us. I can get discouraged at my failings, but his determination is that he has come to bring peace. Jesus' ministry demonstrated that, and his death and resurrection fulfilled it.

Jesus did everything necessary for us to be free, forgiven and completely united with the vibrant person of God. I was fascinated to read today about the Passion Translation's rendition of the words of Jesus on the cross, usually translated, 'It is finished', but in the Passion Translation, 'It is finished, my bride!' (John 19:30). Brian Simmons, who contributed to the Passion Translation, writes that the word 'finished, completed', *kalah*, also carries the meaning 'bride', and so we have a rich picture of Jesus being united with his bride (the church) by his fulfilment of God's purpose on the cross.

Through this peaceful unity between Jesus and the members of his church, we can know God's hopes for us: that his peace will saturate us and flow through us; that it will be on display for the benefit of all. Our momentary failings are nothing compared to God's stunning plan to reveal himself to the world.

'The Word became flesh and made his dwelling among us. We have seen his glory, the glory of the one and only Son, who came from the Father, full of grace and truth' (John 1:14).

VICTORIA BYRNE

God's confidence

'Though the mountains be shaken and the hills be removed, yet my unfailing love for you will not be shaken nor my covenant of peace be removed,' says the Lord, who has compassion on you. (NIV)

I grew up in very flat country, so it always seems very romantic and wonderful to look out of the window and see a line of hills. When I have lived or holidayed among hills, I have loved being able to see land from a distance, to appreciate the different skyline and to see more easily somewhere that is distinctly different from where I am. A hill in the distance often looks like a smooth, rising contour, reassuringly continuous and evenly shaped. Up close, however, hills are so often revealed to be uneven, rocky, scarred by changes and uniquely themselves.

I find the same is true of other people's lives. A person's story can be easy to encapsulate when we don't know them well, but the more I get to know them, they seem more complicated and it's harder to label them or generalise. Everyone has their own interesting complexity. I find it helpful to understand other people's lives, in books or in conversation. It shakes me out of assumptions and generalisations, and wakes me up to realities in my own life.

Where does peace come into this? The challenge of helping others is that the complexities we are confronted with can be overwhelming. How can we begin to help? I'm comforted by these verses, in which God, who knows everything in all its complexity, promises that even if life gets complicated for us, he will still be at peace, and we can share in that. Jesus doesn't ignore our troubles, but he is not brought down by them. He comes and sits with us, as it were, in the midst of them, if we let him. God is always stable. His word brings us back to his unchanging steadfastness.

What area of your life might the Lord be shaking or rebuilding at the moment? How might Isaiah describe the jewels with which he will rebuild?

VICTORIA BYRNE

Peace through Christ

God raised us up with Christ and seated us with him in the heavenly realms in Christ Jesus, in order that in the coming ages he might show the incomparable riches of his grace, expressed in his kindness to us in Christ Jesus. (NIV)

I have been reading through Matthew's gospel recently, thinking about the great arc of the disciples' experience. It has helped me understand something about the work of the cross and our part as Jesus' followers. This is the basis of our peace with God.

The disciples are first called by Jesus in the midst of their working lives, on the lakeshore, dealing with the nets at the water's edge, hauling fish. Straight away they follow him as disciples. They literally follow him to Jerusalem and to the point of crucifixion. Scripture teaches us that as followers of Jesus, we have spiritually followed him to death on the cross and through resurrection as well. By inviting him to be alive in us, we are alive in him – spiritually inseparable from him, so that what happened to Jesus is applied also to us. As such we benefit from his breaking through the barriers of sin and death, and we follow him into God's throne room; we're seated with Christ.

I like to imagine Jesus breaking through some kind of physical barrier (you can pick your favourite), and so as followers united with him, we get to follow in his wake. He is pulling each of us through, like the great rescuer he is.

Jesus effectively tells his followers, 'Now you are on my team, where I go, you go.' He went to Jerusalem, and he overcame death. The Father has graciously chosen to let us be fully united with Jesus; he says we are in his inner circle; he hides us under his wing; he embraces us, and in his broad embrace he takes us with him through death and into a bright place.

Thank you, Lord, that you called me once, and now I am yours. Thank you that my salvation doesn't depend on me being perfect or impressing you. Help me live in the light of that grace.

VICTORIA BYRNE

Steadying our focus on Christ

Christ Jesus: who, being in very nature God, did not consider equality with God something to be used to his own advantage; rather, he made himself nothing by taking the very nature of a servant, being made in human likeness. (NIV)

My focus on peace for the past few weeks has made me aware of all the times when I do not have a peaceful attitude to things and people in my own life. In attempting to work on that, more and more, I have started to feel that we cannot achieve peacefulness by striving for it.

I'm not sure that mere peacefulness is a goal that Jesus would have worked for. His mind was fixed on following what his Father was doing and getting involved with that. Peace was a by-product. I am beginning to think that seeking to achieve peacefulness, and even to provoke that seeking in others, is not a useful goal in itself. I think it easily leads to my adopting a critical mindset towards myself and others, and that is a sure enemy of peace that eats away at the very thing I am trying to achieve.

God's word says, 'Just as he who called you is holy, so be holy in all you do' (1 Peter 1:15), but we also know that only God is perfect. The word tells us to put on the breastplate of righteousness (Ephesians 6:14), and that's provided by God. We put on his righteousness like clothing.

Today's extraordinary passage helps me unpick my thoughts by reminding me that I am following Jesus, who was perfect but chose to focus on serving others, and God. What I particularly love about these verses is that as Paul fixes our attention on Jesus, his thoughts lead naturally to joy; a joy that was shared by Jesus because the joy of union between us and the Father was his purpose in service. So we fix our eyes back on the one who gloriously deserves our gaze.

Who are the people God is inviting you to serve in his name today? Pray for them.

VICTORIA BYRNE

We're being looked after

My help comes from the Lord, the Maker of heaven and earth. He will not let your foot slip – he who watches over you… will neither slumber nor sleep. (NIV)

I was listening today to a radio programme about babies laughing. It was reported that the key factor is the sense of security and connection with the parent. There followed a series of short recordings of babies giggling and laughing. Their laughter was infectious.

We are designed to flourish best when we feel safe. We laugh best when we're unafraid. We learn to take risks when we feel secure. We grow best when we're given challenges but the risks are well managed. Great teachers, mentors and parents do that well; God is the supreme caregiver.

This psalm is a comforting meditation on God's permanent presence around us. This 'song of ascent' was sung as worshippers climbed up Temple Mount towards the place of God's holy presence. It also functions as an allegorical meditation on how God relates to us as we journey through our lives, drawing us ever closer to him.

Whether you are in the midst of a challenge or, like me, completing one and feeling a little anxious about the next, we all benefit from the reminder of God's desire and ability to protect and bless us.

Let's celebrate these truths together. Verse 2: our heavenly Father is powerful, creative and understands the context of our challenges because he created them. Verse 3 reminds us that God cares about us enough to pay careful attention to our well-being and to ensure that he does all he can to prevent our destruction. His protection is not limited by situation, geography or time (vv. 5–8).

No one takes better care of us than God. It is a comfort to know that when we turn in for the night, we can hand worries over to the one who 'neither slumbers nor sleeps'.

What single memento of this journey through peace would you like to take with you as you travel onward?

VICTORIA BYRNE

Enabling all ages to grow in faith

Anna Chaplaincy
Living Faith
Messy Church
Parenting for Faith

The Bible Reading Fellowship (BRF) is a Christian charity that resources individuals and churches. Our vision is to enable people of all ages to grow in faith and understanding of the Bible and to see more people equipped to exercise their gifts in leadership and ministry.

To find out more about our ministries, visit

brf.org.uk

Recommended reading

Green Reflections
Reflecting on our environment with faith
Martin and Margot Hodson
978 1 80039 068 3 £8.99
brfonline.org.uk

How should we look after the world we inhabit? Martin and Margot Hodson bring together scientific and theological wisdom to offer 62 reflections inspired by passages from the Bible in a thoughtful exploration that encourages both reflection and response. Themes include 'The Wisdom of Trees', 'Landscapes of Promise' and 'Sharing Resources'. With original artwork by Martin Beek.

Babies and Toddlers
Nurturing your child's spiritual life
Rachel Turner
978 1 80039 000 3 £4.99
brfonline.org.uk

Our children's early years are incredibly significant in shaping their mental, emotional and spiritual lives for the future, but how do we sow seeds of faith when they are so tiny? In this book Rachel Turner suggests simple, everyday approaches to help our children connect with the God who knows them. Wherever you are on your faith journey, you can help your child meet and know God, and however young your child is, God loves them and has promises for them.

To order

Online: brfonline.org.uk
Telephone: +44 (0)1865 319700
Mon–Fri 9.30–17.00

Delivery times within the UK are normally 15 working days. Prices are correct at the time of going to press but may change without prior notice.

Title	Price	Qty	Total
Green Reflections	£8.99		
Babies and Toddlers	£4.99		
Day by Day with God (May–Aug 2021) – single copy	£4.75		
Day by Day with God (Sep–Dec 2021) – single copy	£4.75		

POSTAGE AND PACKING CHARGES			
Order value	UK	Europe	Rest of world
Under £7.00	£2.00	Available on request	Available on request
£7.00–£29.99	£3.00		
£30.00 and over	FREE		

Total value of books	
Donation	
Postage and packing	
Total for this order	

Please complete in BLOCK CAPITALS

Title _____ First name/initials _____ Surname _____

Address _____

_____ Postcode _____

Acc. No. _____ Telephone _____

Email _____

Method of payment

☐ Cheque (made payable to BRF) ☐ MasterCard / Visa credit / Visa debit

Card no. ☐☐☐☐ ☐☐☐☐ ☐☐☐☐ ☐☐☐☐ ☐☐☐☐

Expires end ☐☐ M M ☐☐ Y Y Security code* ☐☐☐ Last 3 digits on the reverse of the card

Signature* _____ Date _____ /_____ /_____

*ESSENTIAL IN ORDER TO PROCESS YOUR ORDER

Registered with
FUNDRAISING
REGULATOR

Please return this form to:
BRF, 15 The Chambers, Vineyard, Abingdon OX14 3FE | enquiries@brf.org.uk
To read our terms and find out about cancelling your order, please visit brfonline.org.uk/terms.

The Bible Reading Fellowship (BRF) is a Registered Charity (233280)

SUBSCRIPTION INFORMATION

Each issue of *Day by Day with God* is available from Christian bookshops everywhere. Copies may also be available through your church book agent or from the person who distributes Bible reading notes in your church.

Alternatively you may obtain *Day by Day with God* on subscription direct from the publishers. There are two kinds of subscription:

Individual subscriptions
covering 3 issues for 4 copies or less, payable in advance (including postage & packing).

To order, please complete the details on page 144 and return with the appropriate payment to: BRF, 15 The Chambers, Vineyard, Abingdon OX14 3FE

You can also use the form on page 144 to order a gift subscription for a friend.

Group subscriptions
covering 3 issues for 5 copies or more, sent to one UK address (post free).

Please note that the annual billing period for group subscriptions runs from 1 May to 30 April.

To order, please complete the details on page 143 and return with the appropriate payment to: BRF, 15 The Chambers, Vineyard, Abingdon OX14 3FE

You will receive an invoice with the first issue of notes.

All our Bible reading notes can be ordered online by visiting
brfonline.org.uk/collections/subscriptions

Day by Day with God is also available as
an app for Android, iPhone and iPad
brfonline.org.uk/collections/apps

Follow us on Instagram: **@daybydaywithgod**

All subscription enquiries should be directed to:
BRF, 15 The Chambers, Vineyard, Abingdon OX14 3FE
+44 (0)1865 319700 | enquiries@brf.org.uk

DAY BY DAY WITH GOD GROUP SUBSCRIPTION FORM

> All our Bible reading notes can be ordered online by visiting
> **brfonline.org.uk/collections/subscriptions**

The group subscription rate for *Day by Day with God* will be £14.25 per person until April 2022.

☐ I would like to take out a group subscription for _____ (quantity) copies.

☐ Please start my order with the September 2021 / January 2022 / May 2022* issue. I would like to pay annually/receive an invoice* with each edition of the notes. (*delete as appropriate)

Please do not send any money with your order. Send your order to BRF and we will send you an invoice.

Name and address of the person organising the group subscription:

Title _____ First name/initials _____ Surname _____

Address _____

_____ Postcode _____

Telephone _____ Email _____

Church _____

Name and address of the person paying the invoice if the invoice needs to be sent directly to them:

Title _____ First name/initials _____ Surname _____

Address _____

_____ Postcode _____

Telephone _____ Email _____

Please return this form to:
BRF, 15 The Chambers, Vineyard, Abingdon OX14 3FE | **enquiries@brf.org.uk**

To read our terms and find out about cancelling your order, please visit **brfonline.org.uk/terms**.

The Bible Reading Fellowship is a Registered Charity (233280)

DAY BY DAY WITH GOD INDIVIDUAL/GIFT SUBSCRIPTION FORM

To order online, please visit **brfonline.org.uk/collections/subscriptions**

☐ I would like to give a gift subscription (please provide both names and addresses)
☐ I would like to take out a subscription myself (complete your name and address details only once)

Title _____ First name/initials _____ Surname _____

Address _____

_____ Postcode _____

Telephone _____ Email _____

Gift subscription name _____

Gift subscription address _____

_____ Postcode _____

Gift subscription (20 words max. or include your own gift card):

_____

_____

Please send *Day by Day with God* beginning with the September 2020 / January 2021 / May 2021 issue (*delete as appropriate*):

(*please tick box*)	UK	Europe	Rest of world
1-year subscription	☐ 18.00	☐ £25.95	☐ £29.85
2-year subscription	☐ £35.10	N/A	N/A

Optional donation to support the work of BRF £ _____

Total enclosed £ _____ (cheques should be made payable to 'BRF')

Please charge my MasterCard / Visa credit / Visa debit with £ _____

Card no. ☐☐☐☐ ☐☐☐☐ ☐☐☐☐ ☐☐☐☐

Expires end ☐☐ ☐☐ Security code* ☐☐☐ Last 3 digits on the reverse of the card

Signature* _____ Date _____/_____/_____

*ESSENTIAL IN ORDER TO PROCESS YOUR ORDER

Please return this form to:
BRF, 15 The Chambers, Vineyard, Abingdon OX14 3FE | **enquiries@brf.org.uk**

To read our terms and find out about cancelling your order,
please visit **brfonline.org.uk/terms**. The Bible Reading Fellowship is a Registered Charity (233280)

BRF

DBDWG0221